Dan O'Brien

THE ANGEL
IN THE TREES

and Other Monologues

Salamander Street

PLAYS

By the Same Author

Plays

The House in Scarsdale: A Memoir for the Stage

The Body of an American

The Cherry Sisters Revisited

The Voyage of the Carcass

The House in Hydesville

The Dear Boy

The Disappearance of Daniel Hand

Key West

"Will You Please Shut Up?"

either/or

An Irish Play

The Last Supper Restoration

Poetry

New Life

Scarsdale

War Reporter

Contents

For Bebe,
our reason for being

THE ANGEL IN THE TREES

MADELINE

I walked everywhere. I had to, I had no car. I never did, never trusted them. Never felt the need to, being a lifelong New Yorker, or thereabouts. And even here, down South, as they say, I worked not far from home through a walk in the woods to a small college campus where I wrote mostly fluff pieces really for the college alumni publication. They called it a magazine. I was new to this town if you called it a town, a postage stamp-sized campus stuck with a cluster of homes, and then the more far flung houses, where I lived, in the woods, alone. I liked it this way. Even those walks at night that could sometimes get quite lonesome. I was often set upon by dogs, though strangely they'd never bite but bark vociferously as if *I* were the one frightening them. A grey fox might slither like a shroud across the road through the high beam of my flashlight. The deer will wait perfectly still in the dark till you step unaware beside them, and then they snort obstreperously and thunder off terrified into the woods. It was wonderful. Sometimes, from afar, across the occasional field, the retreating deer with their white tails bobbing looked more to me like ghost-riders approaching in the moonlight. It certainly could get strange. As it did that night, about nine-thirty, I believe, my usual time to walk home (I preferred to work late mornings into evening), the oval disk of my flashlight skimming across the surface of the dirt road. When I heard the sound of something falling, a crackling through branches and then a thud like I thought a body might sound, hitting the ground. Though I've never heard such a thing, have you? I threw my beam to where the sound came from: nothing there but trees. The branches grew loud as if tossed with wind – soughing, I believe is the word – though I couldn't feel a thing on my face or neck or hands. It swelled to a roar, and the night in front of my face grew black, my flashlight made no dint. Then everything went quiet again.

Just as quickly as it had first grown loud. I turned round a bend in the road, climbing uphill, my flashlight swerved in the dark and lit upon, standing in the trees with his eyes upon me: an angel.

I did not know what it was. Never having seen one. I mean – have you?

He looked like a man. His body had its own light, pale, as if passed through water. His hair was black and his skin white. He looked like a victim of drowning. I assumed it was a he because of the nature of his face, his features. But there was something sexless about him, not quite androgynous, but – . I could not see his clothes, the light obliterated all detail, he could have been naked for all I knew. And this light stretched not only out from him but up, like bright strings stretched into the canopy of trees above.

He looked at me like he'd known I was coming. As if he'd been waiting for me all my life.

He neither smiled at me nor glared. He held out his hand, as if he had something to give me. A dog barked close by in the trees – and when I looked again he'd gone.

You should know now that despite a lifelong atheism, or really was it simply a kind of lazy secular agnosticism? this was by no means the first time I'd seen an angel. Or a ghost. Or suffered hallucinations. You see, I still don't know what to call them! I was here in the woods for my health. Not that I ever considered myself truly mentally ill. On my bad days I felt gifted, and when I was healthy I knew I had been sick. I'd been sick in more ways than one.

I'd become divorced, lost my job. All in a few months, everything unraveled. I was sleeping all day, ordering my nonperishable groceries delivered past midnight. I'd have them left in my building at the bottom of the stairs, and late at night while everyone slept I'd slip out my door and spirit them away.

It's not a time I like to talk about much.

I'd been suicidal, without ever attempting. You could say I had simply wanted to die, in a vaguely hopeful sort of way, but that I was not interested in taking responsibility for it myself. And then, one day, out of the blue, as if someone were listening and answering my dark prayers, I discovered I was sick. I had all the popular treatments, recovery was considered doubtful.

Then this man moved in. A roommate. His name, he told me, was Rick. He was handsome, if a bit filthy. He wore blue jeans, a leather jacket. He told me he rode a hog. (I think I had a crush on him.) He treated me well, listening to my problems, holding my hand while I threw up, or sobbing. He came with me to the hospital and sat beside me, stroking my face, and my neck, until I fell asleep.

Then one morning, sitting in our kitchen, over coffee, he reveals to me that his name is not Rick at all but Jesus Christ Son of Man.

Naturally, I was upset. I mean – wouldn't you – ? I was terrified! This man was insane! I had to kick him out, it got ugly. The neighbors all complained when they heard the shouts and sounds of heavy things being thrown about. People called the cops on us. But when they broke down the door they found only me there, alone. Screaming, smashing things up. No one in the building had ever seen nor heard of Rick.

I couldn't call my parents, who were both alive still at the time (I had been an only child). They had not spoken to me, nor me them, in years. My marriage had been the reason. Or not the reason, the latest excuse. They did not want me marrying a non-Jew, they said. Can you imagine? in this day and age? We had stockings growing up at Christmastime! Though, to be fair, their colors had been blue and gold. Chanukah stockings. That's how it was.

And Elliot was Episcopalian like I was a Jew.

But what my parents really meant was they did not like him. Elliot. Did not trust him. They could see what I couldn't.

I married him without inviting them, and years later, after the divorce, after I'd gotten sick and suffered this apparent psychotic break, I found I couldn't call them. I wasn't working at the time. I had no savings left, no insurance. At the hospital I gave them Elliot's number.

Another thing happened at the hospital though, a wonderful, remarkable if somewhat problematic – . The doctors all assumed I was still delusional when I said I'd been suffering from cancer. They could not find a trace of it in me. And subsequent tests bore this out. Over the course of those last few months, roughly the time I'd lived with Rick, I'd been healed.

Now, before that, with Elliot, there'd been the incident in Vermont.

Elliot was a brilliant young Turk of an adjunct professor, so everyone told me, all the time, over and over again. Economic History or History of Economics, I never knew which. Or I knew but I've forgotten. Or I forgot because I never cared enough really. And one summer someone at Columbia loaned us their house in Vermont.

Elliot was to finish his first book up there, the book destined to make him a star in certain very small, very miniscule circles. I was between careers. I had been an intellectual, a neophyte with feminist ambitions, and Elliot and I had fallen in love, as they say, in grad school. But it took me five years to finish my dissertation on Neglected Female Poets of the Revolutionary War Era (just a working title), and when I finished I didn't care much for poets, of any gender, any era. I had grown to find academic pursuit inhuman somehow.

Right away I did not have a peaceful sense. There was something in that house in Vermont, in the woods surrounding, that made my skin crawl. Literally. Sometimes the back of your neck will heat up as if someone were touching it with a very warm spoon, or their fingers, perhaps? Well, that was what it was like. Elliot didn't feel a thing. I was suburban bourgeois, he said. It was silence, the peace and the quiet – all that is anathema to the native New Yorker – *that* was what frightened me so. "You're scared of your self!" he'd say. "You're afraid to be alone." And he'd laugh, and hold me. "Ghosts appear only to those who want to see them, Madeline." (I thought he was missing the point, and the definition, of a haunting.) "Do what I do," he'd say, "say it loud: I don't believe in you, ghosts!"

When I was scared of anything, he'd speak to me this way. (He'd made it clear, before we married, that he didn't want to be a father.)

So I said, after him, I don't know why: "I don't believe in you, ghosts!" And he laughed, and let me go.

The problem, you see, as I saw it then, as I see it now, was that I at least a *little* bit believed in ghosts. I mean, don't you? Have you seen one? I'm not ashamed of it now. I often wondered at the time, inwardly, if I were just the smallest bit psychic. You know? I'd been so as a child. I'd seen people in my room, as I drifted off to sleep. Old folks mainly, sitting in outdoor chairs indoors, in my bedroom. It was funny. Or leaning up against my bureau, checking his ghostly pocket watch. In the house when we moved up from the city to the suburbs, this was when I was ten, for months I'd hear an accordion playing each night around bedtime. The same fractured tune, same misplaced breathing. Sometimes just the breath in the breathing box, I think that's what you call it, no melody, as if an extremely ungifted child, asthmatic probably, were laboring to learn it. Like he'd be punished for not playing. My parents did not like music. They were book people.

That house in Vermont I remember was like a ship, an ark really, left high on the mountainside. Four stories up with a cupola like a crow's nest on top of this really insanely steeply pitched roof. It was enormous for us, it swallowed us whole. It had been built, we had been told, by a painter named Galiel in the early 1800s. Galiel had been a merchant sailor, then a spice trader in New York. Then after his wife died he found he liked to paint. His paintings were of the sea: shipwrecks, romantically imagined, beautiful shafts of light like ruined Doric columns toppling into tempestuous waves. He'd had a dozen children, Galiel, the thirteenth having died with that wife in labor. The family that lived there now, during summers and holidays (they were away on sabbatical, in Rome), left most everything they owned behind. So you could say the house was haunted by this family too.

We were sitting on the porch overhanging a ravine. The summer evening was almost preternaturally quiet. I was reading Renan's *Life of Jesus* – have you read it? It's good, it makes Jesus more of a man somehow. I'm no born-again but for some reason I'd always wanted to read this book, and now that I'd given up all academic pursuit I found I could read whatsoever my heart desired, and my heart desired the *Life of Jesus*. Anyway, just when I got to that point where Renan says, you know, that, "Miracles are what *never* happen" (emphasis mine), I paused to think about that. I put the book aside, and I noticed how quiet it had grown. I was about to remark to Elliot how peculiar this absence of wind or cricket or cicada – when we heard an infant cry. Inside our house, upstairs. An *infant*. (It would have been easy to go and find out which room if only we'd been brave.)

Elliot lifted his face from his book.

Ten seconds or so of crying ... Then the crickets in the woods again.

He was quick to dismiss it as a kind of aural illusion: If life can play tricks on the eyes, then why not the ears? especially considering the ear is so impressionable an organ ...

(He actually said that: "an organ.")

And besides, the architecture of the house *was* spooky.

Here we were, alone in the woods, tens of miles from any other human living beings – we were city folk! and the wind (that old saw) or some dying animal in our innocence we could not name nor recognize – it was a sound of nature, he concluded, caught in the echo chamber of our house. (Our house that was not ours.)

Or maybe the animal was *in* the house, in the walls, dying? He admitted there was a possibility of that.

But it was not *like* an infant's cry – it *was* an infant *crying*.

The other time I'd been alone he'd gone down to New York for the day to give a paper, and because I'd begged he was driving home that night. I tried to wait up but fell asleep with the lights on (I always slept with the lights on when I was alone).

And I woke in the middle of the night to what sounded like cannonballs – falling on the roof!

Or hail the size of bread loaves, large rocks falling from the sky – and falling on the roof!

Can you imagine – the *sound* – ?

I felt – no, I knew, that our house was somehow under attack. As if a ship at sea, or in a storm, we were foundering on the rocky shoal.

I opened up the front door: no hail, no stones from the sky.

I ran to the stairs – I was not going to let this one get away, not this time – and still waking up I climbed to the second floor, the third – .

There were maid- and butler-quarters up there, long neglected into storage rooms, full of junk, memories, all covered in dust like moss.

The crashing tumult continued above my head.

I imagined people up there now, like something out of Dante, very strange souls, very strong, like angels, or demons – beating their fists on the roof.

So up the stairs to the fourth and highest floor I ran, and switching on the hall lights as I flew, switching on every light in every room I passed – every door flung wide, the rooms staring back at me, furniture and crazy stacks of books and records, boxes, empty clothes and piles of damaged children's toys – "What are you looking for?" "There's no one here but you."

I stood in the hallway, as the roof and walls around me shook. Pummeled. I spoke from the bottom of myself in a voice I did not know I had: "*I do not believe in you, ghosts!*"

It's funny. It worked. The sound and shaking stopped.

You know, I felt something surprising in that moment: they'd listened to me, whoever they were. Galiel the painter, his long-dead, long-birthing wife, their children. The sailors whose ghosts he'd entombed in those shipwreck paintings. The thirteenth child, who'd cried that other night for ten seconds long. "Thank you," I said quietly, to all of them. I turned out all the lights.

Naturally Elliot didn't understand. I told him when he came home. I had to, because you see I met him at the door and burst into tears right away. I cried, stupidly. I was happy, I insisted. ("Happy about what?") He brushed past me up the stairs, two at a time, inspected that fourth floor, even climbing up into the cupola and finding nothing there but a window pane diagonally split – he hadn't noticed that before – "*There*," I said – "that's your proof!" And he looked at me for the first time with fear in his eyes.

No, not fear …

It wasn't long before he told me he was in love with someone else. He used that word, he thought it made it better somehow.

So you could say I had experience with ghosts. But I did not yet know what I believed.

It was my idea to move south, after the divorce, and after cancer and Rick, my Hell's Angels Christ. I wasn't going to call what happened to my cancer a miracle. As Renan says, miracles are what never happen. It was the power of a desperate mind that had brought Rick to me, in order to help me heal myself. (I was Jewish, so how could I believe in Rick?)

The town I chose for myself is called Lowden. Which is an odd name, I'll grant you, considering how high atop a rocky plateau it sits: it catches the passing clouds like the head of a nail in a fence might snag a passing thread. And sometimes the clouds stick around for days, weeks even. A month of untempered grey is not unheard of. And really it isn't cloudy all the time but fog is the norm when the air is damp, and the air is always damp because, you see, Lowden is in the clouds.

The plateau looks like a mountain range that's been cut off at the waist, or knees. As if God shaped the landscape with a sword.

Sometimes, in a storm, lightning ripples synaptically through the fog and trees ... silently: no thunder.

The town was founded in 1834 by a group of religious fanatics from upstate New York (of course, you say). The Lowdenites, as they came to be rather ungracefully known, were Utopians who believed in free living, but not free love. In fact they abhorred the body so much so that, like so many Utopians before and after, they dribbled out unto extinction. Then Lowden became a copper mining town, and persisted in poverty for decades.

And then one day at the end of the century, an heiress to a copper mining magnate came up the mountain to visit this town where so many of her father's miners had lived and died. Guilt may have been her inspiration, or father-hatred, who knows? This woman had faith. Even at a young age her family and friends saw in her the violent light of zealotry. But she had not yet found her cause.

Until she came up to Lowden. And lo, the story, as I have heard it, as I have had cause to recycle it ceaselessly in the Lowden College Alumni Magazine, was that this woman fell in love with this place. She loved the clouds, the plateau in fog. And most of all she loved the trees. There is a spirit in the trees, I imagine her saying. And people would've simply laughed at her if she hadn't had the money to put where her mouth was. She bought the town, built the college, raised twelve churches all of varied Christian faiths (roughly one church for every fifty souls in those days). She was absolutely, and unequivocally, insane. She often said she did not care what one was, so long as one believed.

Now, it's true, that being Jewish by birth I felt sometimes somewhat out of place here. To say that I had not lived a religious life up until this point would not be entirely false modesty. My sins were many. I did not like old people, which I knew might become more and more problematic as I grew older. I'd never liked babies, and yes I believe there's some overlap there with the old. And you know already something of my problematic relationship to dogs, and in truth pets or wildlife in general (I am not an outdoorsy person, let us just say).

And then there were the varying degrees of immoralities, sexual and otherwise, thank you very much, at any given time, at different points in my life, though not nearly enough points lately.

And also there was what happened with my parents, how they both died at once. Of mercy killing, euthanasia, I guess you call it. Suicide. They did it together, which was so like them. And I didn't find out until they'd been buried two months.

In Dante, though I am no Dante scholar – English is my only language – American, I should say – in the fifth circle of Hell you will find the depressives buried in the marshy black waters of the River Styx. I remember reading that not too long ago, and it astounded me: I had not known you could go to Hell for that. For being "sullen," was I think the word used: Grim and sullen in the sunlit air, to paraphrase. And so these sullen souls are buried deep within the viscous mud, and their sighs are bubbles breaking the surface slime.

(I sigh all the time. It's often how I breathe.)

And above them, trapped in the very same mud, waist-deep like pigs, or larvae, are the wrathful, those that lived a life of fury. As if anger toward others is slightly better than anger toward oneself.

I don't know how I feel about all that …

But Christian Lowden suited me just fine. Like the copper mining magnate's daughter, I felt the spirit in the woods too. I did, when I visited, years ago with Elliot on academic retreat. I'd hit it off well with a professor's wife named Nancy, and Nancy edited the Lowden College Alumni Magazine. So after my divorce and illness and breakdown and so-called miraculous healing, without mentioning any of that, I picked up the phone and gave Nancy a ring.

"You don't look so hot," she said.

We'd been discussing a feature on this one-legged rock climber, a student. We both said we found it inspiring.

I said I thought I should go home. I had a migraine.

"I didn't know you got migraines!" she said, as if I'd just told her I macraméd (good for you!).

The truth was I didn't get migraines anymore, not since Rick. I was scared, that's all, intrigued, let us say, by my vision of the angel. I'd passed that spot on the way in this morning where I'd seen him the night before: a weedy rise beside a dead or dormant tree. The grass where the angel had stood was not even downpressed: it flared up in a weedy thatch, shreds of leaves tangled in the brush.

On the way back home, it was hardly past noon, the fog was falling in. I was used to walking in it. I liked how it could open up your ears to things and help you hear the world as if peripherally, if not in three hundred and sixty degrees. The leftover raindrops rolling from a twig to the flat palm of a leaf below. The dogs as always barking behind that striated wall of trees (what were they saying to each other, across such vast distance?). A train whistling even farther off than that, one high pitched cliché sustained, not so much foreboding as nostalgic, elegiac. But mostly it was the raindrops I liked listening to.

A car flashed round the bend – no headlights. A student, I could tell, at the wheel of her white SUV. I slopped down into a ditch, and tried my best to glare up through the driver's side window. I was not noticed.

What is it about these girls and their SUVs? I assumed it was a girl, I don't know why. And almost all of them drove these really very enormous cars purchased for their safety by their fathers. They sit high behind the wheel, like a princess on a stallion, or carried in a livery by slaves.

Someone stood in the road, near where I'd seen the angel. Through the fog he was just a shape.

"Tricky turn," he called out to me.

The angel held a leash in his hand. The dog, this fat mud-colored spaniel, barked at my approach.

"I ought to carry a flashlight – like you." He chuckled. "When will I ever learn?"

This was Walter Tawwater. Say that name, you can't help but sound Southern. I'd met him a handful of times on the road these past months. We'd never stopped to speak really but pattered on instead like neighbors might, in passing, about the weather, the winter population of deer, a rabid raccoon rumored dead nearby.

He was a small man, old. And something in the bones of his face made him look half-demented: sharp cheeks and a jutting, delicate chin – a lecher, that was the word that sprang to mind. Or maybe he was ill. Have I mentioned how ancient he was? Harmless, I thought, as the dog barked, its eyes befuddled by cataracts, froth looping from its chin.

"You should get yourself a flashlight," I said as I passed, smiling (was I flirting?) – "for safety's sake!"

He laughed again in that false fatherly way, and yanked the dog's bark out of it. He took a step or two up from the road, into that grassy patch that was this morning untouched.

For this reason, I stopped.

"Everything fine?" asked Walter Tawwater. He smiled, his dentures were bright, a beacon in the fog.

I switched my flashlight off.

"You live around here, right?"

He nodded. "Up that way." He pointed through an overhang of branches.

"Have you ever seen anyone out here? – alone, at night?"

"Besides you?" He laughed again. It was a nervous spasm, breathless. I thought maybe he had emphysema, like my father.

The dog barked again as if to mask his master's cough.

"What I mean is, do you ever see men out here?"

He looked at me, baffled, his fist before his mouth.

"Why? What've you seen?"

"I don't know."

"Well you'd best be careful. There's a pervert on the loose." He said the word like *pre*-vert. "There's some prevert creeping round, exposing himself to girls who go walking in the woods, alone, at night."

The way he smiled looked as though he thought the girls deserved it.

In the fall there had been a rape of a girl. They'd never caught the rapist. It caused a stir on campus, as it should, and in the community where there had been not one documented violent crime since before the churches were built. I wondered if I was a girl, from Walter Tawwater's point of view.

"Okay," I said. "Thanks for the warning." And I switched back on my light. The fog was drifting through the trees in soft, smoke-like folds.

Walter Tawwater jerked his dog's head up out of the grass: its nose had uncovered a dead snake like a small white stick.

"You'd best be careful," he repeated his warning: "Otherwise you might find yourself *exposed* to!" and he laughed again, that wheezing spasm. I thought to myself, just for a moment, that clearly Walter Tawwater was the prevert of whom he spoke.

When I looked over my shoulder to see if he'd gone, he was still there, still watching me through the fog. His dog had turned his back on both of us, barking at something in the trees I couldn't see.

***

What was the angel holding in his hand?

That was what kept me up at night, or most of that first and second night. I had to rely on sleeping pills, a drink or two, or three. Or four. And checking several times that every window and every door was locked. And my brass fire poker in bed beside me (sleeping with my poker) as had been my habit for some time now, as a woman, as a girl, living alone here in a dark wood full of angels and lechers. (The girl who'd been raped in the fall had been jogging not far from my house.) Because how did I know it was an angel I had seen at all and not a man? some flesh-and-blood prevert like Walter Tawwater?

And if not a man how did I know it was an angel? Why was I so sure? It could have been a devil, a demon of some kind. Or just your run-of-the-mill ghost. A haunting, and nothing special about it at all.

What's the difference between a ghost story and a God story anyway?

Do you know?

What *was* he holding in that hand ... ?

You see, because even when I was sick, I did not believe. I did not believe in God. As they say.

I wanted to – in foxholes and hospitals, etc. – but it always felt somehow somewhat somewhere out there beyond me. Beyond my powers. Of what? I did not have that gift. That's what I used to think. You have it or you do not. Children have it. Naiveté? A friend of mine used to say all the time, "Either you're haunted, or you go to church."

What I had been haunted by, my whole life, if I'm honest with myself, and you, was: what if *neither* is the case: no God, no ghost. What if you reach a certain point in life, a certain age, as I had reached mine, and rather than finding oneself swept up in a desperate certitude of the facts of the things of the kingdom of the world to come – what if at this point you see what is *truly* horrific about life: that there is nothing there behind it all at all?

It's like you're walking in the woods alone at night. Your flashlight is your mind, forever casting out, fishing out into the black, piercing the caul of night with your one thin beam, your narrow mind, your little subjective life, and seeing only maybe that step or two in front of you, as we all do, as all of us are guilty of … Maybe once in the odd while you cast your light out to the left or to the right, out into the wide landscape – you're ambitious, brave, you're desperate – and little bits of things appear, snatches of fragments of things – things that are *true*. Most of the time it's just the trees you see. But maybe, you think, maybe one day, your beam will light upon a face.

I lay awake in bed waiting for the fog of Nembutal to descend. This house I was renting was only maybe ten years old, no one had died here yet. Outside, wind chimes, rain gushed gently round the eaves and down through new copper gutter pipes. I was alone in the world. I felt somehow my plan was now almost complete. Not Elliot, nor what was left of my family – no one knew where I was, what had become of me. No one who had ever known me could be said to know me now. And no one who knew me now had any idea who I was.

I pulled the pillow over my face and slept.

The next day Nancy drove me to The Piggly Wiggly (or The Pig, as we call it – the locals do) like she did every Friday before picking her kids up at school. We talked pleasantly about nothing: that one-legged rock climber would have the cover this month, there'd been no unequivocal sun since Valentine's Day, Nancy's husband Don was experiencing an emergent hemorrhoid.

"Have you ever seen a ghost?" Maybe it was all this talk about the weather. I tried to make the question sound playful, daring.

"No!" she said, half-astonished (she was so cute). "Why do you ask? Have *you* seen a ghost?" And she sneaked a peek at me.

I answered in all sincerity that "Yes, I've seen one or two in my day."

The windshield wipers clacked uselessly. The windshield was an almost perfect pane of water. Nancy swerved minutely in her lane.

"I've seen ghosts a lot," I pressed on. "Or I should say I've seen some ghosts, and I've heard others."

(I didn't mean to sound defensive.)

"I think it's beautiful." And I left it there.

On the way home, Nancy's minivan full of food, for me but also for Nancy and her hemorrhoidal husband and their four darling kids, Nancy asked, "Have you ever heard of the Angel of Lowden?"

My God. I had not. *Had* I?

"It's a legend, a local kind, about an angel that guards the mountain."

"From what?"

"Sorry?"

"What does the angel guard the mountain from?"

"Oh, I don't know. Evil, I guess."

"And is it a Christian angel?"

"Now what do you mean by that?" she was laughing again, as if I were making some kind of red-state, blue-state joke. (I wondered if she knew I had been raised a kind of Jew.)

"Is it a Christian or a Jewish or a Muslim angel or what?"

She flicked her turn signal, glancing into her mirror, as we exited the interstate.

"Christian. It would have to be, down here, wouldn't it?"

On the side of the road we passed a tow truck with orange lights revolving. It maneuvered to lift a wrecked compact car that was black, burned out. There was no one inside that I could see.

At the house Nancy insisted on helping me with the groceries, as she did every week. And every week I said No it's all right, I got it, Nancy. But this week for some reason I let her come in. I was slovenly these days. I'd yet to have anyone over on any very social terms. I hadn't decorated, per se. My laundry, clean and soiled and all shades between, occupied two easy chairs and half of my new sofa. Boxes sat open-mouthed on the foyer floor. I had killed a spider with a dictionary, days ago, and the book lay on the carpet still, the spider dead beneath it.

"Are you all right, Madeline?" I thought she meant my groceries.

She waited, frozen, deer-like, in the middle of my kitchen. She put her hand on mine, on the countertop. I made a fist.

"I'm fine," I said. I laughed. No one had said my name in a very long time. It didn't sound like my name.

"I only ask because – "

"Do I seem *not* okay to you?"

"No, that's not it. I only meant if *I* was living out here, all alone, without Don … " She was shaking her head at me as if she admired me. Or maybe it was pity.

After the silence, we laughed some more. All around us the week's groceries seemed to exhort us on to more practical concerns. We made some disparaging remarks about men, and Nancy said she'd love a month or two away from Don and this ubiquitous hemorrhoid of his ("all men are babies," she said – she actually said that! "Babies!"). And I walked her to the door and thanked her for the ride, for carrying my groceries in, "Good night, Nancy, have a nice weekend, I'll see you Monday morning."

That night I called Elliot. I would've thought our phone number would of course now be long defunct (we had not spoken in years), but a woman answered:

"Elliot?" she said, not to me but out behind herself, back into the apartment. (She sounded very sober, very cautious. Elegant.) He lived on Riverside. It had been his mother's apartment, so in the split of course he'd kept it, along with all our friends, strangely. He taught at Columbia still, walked to the same subway stop, unless there was sun and then he walked all the way up, through the park. He loved that park, along the river, the big trees. He loved to walk. It was the one hobby we shared, besides books. I remember the apartment perfectly. I walk through it in my mind. I haunt it.

He picked up: "Yeah."

This was how he always answered: as if he were only slightly ticked to be interrupted in the midst of some profound yet workmanlike abstraction, rubbing the strain from his eyes with ink-stained fingertips (he preferred to write longhand, of course, the prick). I was shocked he could still sound so much the same.

"Elliot, it's Madeline Singer."

Isn't that hilarious? that I felt the need to give him my last name … (This would've been harder had I been sober.)

"Hi!" he said, as if excited to hear from me. It died out like that: "Hi … !"

"How are you?"

"Where are you calling me from?"

"The South."

The phone line hissed and crackled. Did he want me to be more specific?

"Wow," he said. Then, "Why?"

(Did he mean why the South? why call?)

"I moved here last year. In the fall. It's been great for me. Really great. I've always wanted to move down south."

"You have? Since when? I didn't know that."

"Yeah."

"I did not *know* that."

"I know you didn't but it's true, Elliot. I like things better down here. Things are slower down here."

"I've heard that."

"Things are, I don't know, more real."

"Real? In what way?" And there it was again: that old condescending cocksuredness.

I said, "People are kinder here."

"Isn't that where they, like, invented slavery, the South?"

"You know what I mean: people are honest. Unlike New York. They're giving, less judgmental. They're not snobs."

His silence meant he was insulted. Which was intended.

"I hate New York now," I added.

"You do?"

"Is that so hard to believe?"

"Are you alone?"

"Yes. Are you jealous?"

"What I mean is are you living down there by yourself?"

"So?"

It sounded like he was walking into another room.

"It's a spiritual place too," I added, "the South."

And against my better judgment I heard myself telling him the story of the Angel of Lowden. How it inhabited the air above the foggy plateau. How it protected the townspeople from evil.

"What kind of evil are we talking about here, Mad?"

(I'd always found this an unfeminine nickname, an unfortunate pun.)

"Mad?"

"I don't know, Elliot. Any kind of evil. You know, despair is a sin. I read that."

And because he didn't respond right away, I told him what I'd seen.

"An angel."

"Yes. Standing on the side of the road only two nights ago. I saw him with my own eyes. It was fantastic! I wasn't dreaming – he was looking right at me."

I heard him whisper something: he was cupping the mouthpiece and speaking in very measured tones, trying for reassuring.

(Was that a child I heard crying in the other room? in the kitchen?)

"Madeline? Are you okay?" (That question again!)

"How do you mean?"

"Do you think you're healthy? Because if you don't mind me saying so I think you sound – . Have you been depressed?"

"Do you mean am I grim and sullen in the sunlit air? The answer's no, not really."

"What are you talking about?"

"I'm not ill, Elliot. I'm not depressed. I'm happy! Happier than I've ever been in my entire fucking life!"

I heard his breath. The rhythm of it shallow, repressed, like always. I closed my eyes and for a moment I could smell him.

"Don't call me again. Okay?"

"Ever?"

"Not when you're drinking."

"I'm not drinking – I'm not drinking *now*."

I heard myself cackle, like a witch, like an old hollowed-out witch. He'd made love to me when I was a girl. So I asked him:

"Why didn't you believe me?"

"Why didn't I believe you about what?"

"When you were gone and I heard those people on the roof of the house in Vermont. When I thought the house was like a ship at sea. Or before that, the baby crying. Why didn't you believe me when I told you I was scared?"

Behind his hand that woman's voice again. I heard the word "soft," and her tone was critical.

He spoke again: "We should stop – "

I hung up.

That night I dreamed of the angel. He looked the same but he held a sword. He had no apparent wings, or wings like a hummingbird maybe, fluttering too fast to see as he hovered there above me, above the naked trees. I saw him through the branches, his bright body set out against starlight, as he walked upon the treetops, like pinpoints, from twig to twig his almost womanly feet brought no weight. His sword was liquid, like a lash of silver it dangled to the ground. And I climbed it, cutting my wrists and hands – I was with him in the trees. My hands and wrists and arms and legs were sliced like mouths. I balanced there on a high branch, sinking and just about to fall – when he reached out his hand to me.

The next morning the sky was blue. Clear skies had been augured in my dream.

It was spring. Somehow. Overnight. And despite all that bright sunshine, air warm and fat with pollen, what concerned me most this morning – for some reason I was worried – was what the angel might be protecting me from.

If he were protecting me at all.

What was out there, exactly, for me to be so frightened of?

Maybe Elliot and Nancy were right: I was not well. Maybe I was sick again.

But instead of the doctor I went to the library.

The Lowden College library is small and almost always infested with geriatrics. I couldn't find any books of local lore. I read some things about angels in general, of all kinds, all religions, but I found the topic multifarious to a fault. I asked the librarian, a thick, Amishy-looking young man, and he asked me back, as if I were joking, "*What* kind of lore?"

"Local. You know, ghost stories mainly." I smiled, coquettishly, weirdly. "Maybe something about angels?"

"Angels?"

This old bitch at the paperback rack scowled in my direction. Other folks were listening now too.

"Well, what you ought to do is go talk to Walter Tawwater … "

I asked him to say that name again.

"Taw-water. He collects ghost stories and stuff. Legends. He used to work here. But he didn't have his certificate. He got fired, or retired. Who knows? You might call Walter an amateur folk-loricist – I know *he* would!"

The young man lowered his voice and leaned in across the countertop, and maybe he winked (it could have been a twitch): "Best you watch yourself around Walter though. He's a real ladies' man. A *dog*."

Outside students were jogging, biking, in shorts or with their shirts off though it couldn't have been more than fifty degrees. I was shocked by their young bodies. Where had they been all winter long? But here they were now, fresh from hiding, pale, reborn and red-cheeked, not all of them attractive or probably smart – some downright ill-equipped for the world, that much was obvious – but all of them beautiful and sweet and sadder than they'll ever know in the simple fact of their youth. I wanted to cry for them. I wanted to speak, to give them some wisdom of some kind, but all I could think worth saying was, You are so lucky. And I knew that was envy. The simple way some of them waved to me – . It broke your heart.

Along one stretch of road, newborn white flowers festooned the high bramble like a presentiment of marriage.

That car came racing down the hill, toward campus again.

I stumbled back down into the shallow ditch again, and again I could not see who was driving. It was the same car, or one just like it: a white SUV. I wondered who it was that lived out here who'd come barreling down along this blind curve on a regular basis like that.

After supper I went out again into the warm twilight and I waited, on the side of the road near the spot where I'd seen the angel only three nights before.

"Christ!" he said, when darkness had come, the fog had returned. "You scared me half to death, standing there like that. I thought you was some kind of *pre*-vert."

He laughed feebly, he coughed. The dog would not bark: it looked drugged. I walked closer.

"I didn't mean to scare you, Mr. Tawwater."

"Walter."

"Okay."

"Why you standing out here all by your lonesome?"

"I was waiting for you."

He cocked his head like a dog.

His house was neat, the furniture worn but clean. Knickknacks and photographs in frames, nature landscapes and Navajo rugs – everything dustless and unsmudged. I was surprised to discover Walter was a neat man. A bachelor? There were no obvious photos of wife or children. The house smelled like potpourri and fried onions. The walls were exposed wood, a log cabin feel.

The dog, as it turned out, was a male named Webb, two B's, and he had free reign here. He sat on the sofa on some brocaded pillows as if waiting to be entertained.

Walter offered me a drink. With his coat off he'd shrunk, as if that were possible. He shuffled, his back hunched, and from time to time he'd adjust his teeth discreetly with his tongue. He dropped ice from tight hands into these brightly cleaned glasses. He poured gin and tonic without asking.

"The Lowden Angel is a stone cold fact. People been seeing her for ages." (Her, I thought, how can that be?) "Even before the Lowdenites came up the mountain, Native Americans known all about her."

"She lives here? On the mountain? Why?"

He brought the drinks to me. They rattled in his claws. I took my glass from him, as he lowered himself beside me, on the couch with effort, and pain, the dog named Webb between us. (Webb had found he liked me now: his head lolled wetly in my lap as I stroked.)

"Angels got to live somewhere," said Walter, and he chuckled, heavily, lifting his glass up: "To angels."

"Is this a holy place?"

His glass stuck to his lip. He looked at me, then the window. I could see my face reflected next to his.

"I don't know nothing about holy." He shrugged and drank.

I drank quickly too, and deeply, and shivered at the numbness on my tongue, the bite in my throat.

He smiled at me, "Whoa there … "

"What's the angel look like?" I asked.

"You ever been in love?"

This shocked me.

"I have. Many times," he said. "It used to be hard on my wife, that I fell in love so often. I kept a lot of things from her. I feel bad about that. But I suppose I got this talent. For loving. You want another?"

I didn't mind. "Where's your wife?" I asked. "Are you divorced?"

He was fixing me my drink. "We don't believe in all that."

"I've never seen her."

"She's dead."

He sat down again, handed me my drink.

He looked a bit jealously at his dog in my lap. Then he grimaced like he tasted something bad.

"She died there." And he pointed without looking, near the TV. "I cared for her."

He was looking back at that black window again. Past his reflection. Webb was twitching in my lap like he was dreaming.

Walter's eyes, in the window, were wet.

"You've been in love before," he said, turning back to me, "I can tell."

Then when I didn't answer: "Got somebody now?"

I thought to explain to him about Elliot. To tell him about all those ghosts up there in Vermont. To mention how Elliot cheated on me because it was probably my fault. I wanted to touch his hand.

"This is nice. I like talking to you," he said.

"I've seen the angel, you know."

"Have you!" He laughed, then coughed into his fist terribly … He sat back on the couch, waiting.

"Three nights ago," I said.

"Three nights? That so?"

"On the side of the road. It was watching me."

Then, as if in confidence, he leaned in again:

"You know, I think I've seen her too."

The dog slithered out of my lap, onto the floor. It disappeared. The room was cold like a window had been opened.

"I've seen her many times, many nights, for many months now. Everyone sees her, walking through the woods, alone, at night."

He held out his hand to me. He was trying to open his fingers.

I let him kiss me. I don't know why. I was drunk, but not really. He tasted like gin. No one had wanted to kiss me in such a long time, I laughed all the way through it.

"What's funny?" I shook my head as if to say, It's not your fault you're old.

When he touched my breast I stood.

"You're the angel!" he called out after me – "Don't you get it? You're the angel, baby!" as I walked down the trail from the house, stumbling in the dark on stones and leaves and dirt. I stepped in mud and thought of Dante. I lost both shoes and kept walking, barefoot. The dog was barking somewhere in the yard behind me. The light from Walter's house was like spears through the branches. I wondered if he'd follow me, if he were a pervert, a rapist. I could outrun him if I had to. I could kill him with my hands. It was sad! the way he talked about his wife. So sad. I was laughing through tears as I walked.

I turned on my light, but it was dead now.

The night was full of fog, no moon. I had a short walk home, I knew it by feel. I had yet to climb the hill.

"You're the angel," he'd said to me. He'd held out his hand.

Headlights came soaring round the bend. Did I move toward or away? I felt it hit. Crush through me like wind and away.

When I got home my front door was wide open. I tried to turn on the lights in the house but found I couldn't. I walked all over. "You're the angel," he'd said.

Someone is here: I look in all the rooms. I hear nothing in my ears. I walk to the bedroom, and he's waiting beside my bed like a bridegroom. He's not angry, or sad. Compassionate or disappointed. It's simply him, his presence, that makes me see that my clothes are torn, I'm no longer holding my flashlight, it's been lost, thrown into the woods by the impact with the car. That I am now wet with blood. My arms and legs and head. That I have in fact stopped bleeding.

He holds his hand out to me: inside he holds that mysterious thing.

BOXING THE COMPASS

North

(Belfast. Bare feet, cigarette. Music stops.)

CONSTANCE

Riall, you stupid fucking Prod. *(Music – a phrase or two on a fiddle.)*

The way you ring the cinema:

"Pardon me, madam, but could you be so kind as to tell me when your next showing might be?" The way you solicit information, the way you colonize. You're like a caricature of yourself when you open your mouth. I hardly recognize you. *(Music.)*

I went with a bloke for a while named Fatch O'Byrne. The lads used to call him Fisheye, for reasons I care not to speculate upon. He never approved of my smoking, Fisheye: be walking down the quay, me smoking my fag right down to the tip and fwip off my fingers and into the wind – "Oh no you don't!" cries Fatch, serious now, "you're gonna' start a fire!" he says, stamping the cinder into concrete, stomp stomp, then spitting for good measure, the mad, mad boy …

He was a Protestant too, Riall.

Said when he was dead he wanted to be hung from a crucifix and suspended aloft at his own bloody wake …

He had some creativity in him all right. *(Music – she interrupts:)*

I'm glad we never married, all the same. *(Music.)*

You know when I knew I was in trouble? It was that year in Canterbury – you were calling from Siberia. The kids had you by the bollocks: "It's hard to teach English to Siberians." – Just cause you're from Belfast doesn't mean Siberia's a fucking holiday, Riall! I tried to tell you. The way you cried on the phone … I never thought I'd grow up to know a man who cried … And I was sitting on my couch – in Canterbury – up the hill from the Cathedral, which absolutely always blew my mind, while you sniveled through the phone from some cement hut in Siberia. And I remember thinking that my couch had become a boat – you know, like you do when you're a child? – tiny boat afloat on the surface of the measureless deep … in danger of breaking … of sinking. I remember saying to myself, Good Christ, Con, what have you got yourself into? *(Silence.)*

I know you love me, Riall. You've said as much. –That's not what I'm on about here. *(Music.)*

El Salvador called. I meant to tell you, but you're never listening. You're never listening. – Shut up, you're not. They want to make me chair of the department. Can you imagine? at my age? Isn't that mad? Aren't you happy? – Will you come? It'd be just like Mexico, without the worms. Remember the worms? Three solid days puking in the jakes. All young lovers should get parasites together. We felt indestructible after that. *(Music.)*

"Horror vacuui." What do you think of that?

One of my students found it – pointed it out to me in class: She said horror vacuui means "fear of emptiness." She said it with that small girl's voice. And when I heard it, I almost cried. Fear of emptiness. It's what map makers named places on the globe they'd never seen: "Horror vacuui." And they filled the empty spaces with pictures of boats, faces of wind, sea-monsters. – Monsters are preferable to nothing. Anything's preferable to the horror vacuui. *(Slight pause.)* That's how I am, isn't it? Always talking, but never saying anything – . What is it I'm afraid of, do you think?

Are you listening to me? *(Music.)*

I love that you love my feet, my toes. That you kiss them. Thanks for doing that. No man's ever done that for me, never. You make me feel like a natural Catholic. My Catholic feet, your Protestant lips. *(Music – she interrupts:)*

Jesus, we're like a fucking metaphor for political healing. *(Music.)*

– The story is, Peary's on his way to the Pole. His servant – a black fellow – takes a knife and slides it down inside the mouth of Peary's boots, cuts the boots from off his feet. Peary's legs are white and bloodless to the knee. And as the servant peels off the painful undershoes that are made of rabbitsfur, several toes from each foot cling to the hide and snap off at the joint. The servant cries aloud, "My God, Lieutenant! Why didn't you tell me your feet were frozen?" And Peary replies, "A few toes aren't much to give to achieve the Pole." *(Silence.)*

I read that to my children on Friday. It's a beautiful story, I think. *(Music.)*

I'm cold. I'm always cold in this room. I should really put some shoes on. *(Music.)*

We fuck well. I mean, we really do fit. That's one thing – a big thing. I'm obsessed with sex. I'm perverted. I masturbate all the time, at least two to three times per week. Once I sniffed your knickers. You should know that about me before we get started. *(Slight pause.)*

… I don't know, Riall … I don't know. *(Music.)*

… You don't know somebody at all, and it's like terra incognita, and then little by little you sail round the Cape of Good Hope, talk to a few Portuguese, someone makes it back from India and now you've got Continents and Oceans and Icebergs and Atolls, and some disappear, and some reappear or appear for the very first time – and so what if South America looks like a hunk of cheese? Antarctica's half the fucking globe? all maps are imperfect, at least at first – but you're *going* somewhere. Right? We've all got to go somewhere eventually … *(Silence.)*

Do you love me?

– Really?

– How do you know we're not wasting our time? *(Music.)*

… You are there, and I am … here. So much could happen in between. *(Music.)*

Would you love me if I were hit by a car? If I were horribly and irrevocably disfigured and you didn't recognize me at all. – If cancer struck, the terrible kind you feel you shouldn't even speak aloud? like bone, blood, lung. – What if I go insane? what if I already am? What if you move in with me and you colonize me and I'm inhospitable country? inhabited by savages? What if to love me you've got to wipe out the entire indigenous population – poison the potatoes and feed me grass till I choke, you stupid fucking Prod how dare you ask me to marry you – ! *(Music – interrupts:)*

I'm not cruel. I'm confused.

I'm lost. It's a big question you've asked me.

I stop for homeless, I give them money, a cigarette. – Why do I do that? *(Silence.)*

– How do you feel?

About this: About what I'm saying.

Tell me again why this is a good idea? *(Silence.)*

I see.

I see.

I love you too.

(Music, then fade.)

South

(Cork. Music. A pub theater.

MORGAN, *in a track suit, shadow-boxing.*

Music & MORGAN *stop on a dime.)*

MORGAN

Surprise. *(Pause.)*

Bet you didn't think I'd be auditioning now did you? I didn't either. Was just something I wanted to do like, had to do, you know so … here I am. I'd like to audition – Jesus this is weird! I mean, I *know* you, I mean – .This is just weird. Like weird-sisters weird. – I want to be Mac – can I say that? is that allowed? Isn't that a theatrical sin or something? like saying "good luck" instead a "break a leg" might set you on fire? Well I've no wish to curse your entire theatrical endeavor before it's even got started, so let's be professional here:

"My name is Morgan O'Donnell, and I am here to audition for the role of the Scottish King." *(Pause.)*

It's funny, I mean when we were, you know, together like – Christ, you saw me naked! on more than one occasion! and I – frankly, Anne, and I hope this doesn't come as a surprise to you: I enjoyed it. The nakedness. For what it's worth. And now I'm scared to death of you! Maybe that's because we're not doing much of that anymore – you know, the nakedness … – Would you mind if I took my pants off? Might help me relax. – No – "Shut up, Morgan." Right, right so. *(Slight pause.)* So: How's things, girl?

Good, glad to hear it. *(Pause.)*

So's I been doing a ton a research. I read the play twice – twice! Don't like to read, as you very well know, a major thorn in our romantic entanglements together. – Basically because nobody talks like that is why I don't care for your man Shakespeare, and on top of it all the fucker's English writing about Scotland and while there's some Scottish in me I think we should be doing an Irish play because that's who we are – . But that's the Catholic Me talking. I mean, you've got to do your art, and that's fair, and "art's" fair – that makes you who you are, Anne. But I've been reading *Mein Kampf*, you know, just to get a handle on what Macbeth is all about and – I said it.

Jesus.

I said: Macbeth.

"Macbeth."

– Macbeth Macbeth Macbeth! There – d'you smell smoke?

– Anyway, I understand your man. You know, wanting something better of my life. You never saw it in me – you never did – because we never really got to know each other at all, or all that well. So I'm not holding nothing against you, girl, but I do want to be better than I am. Who doesn't? I could be a film actor, for example, if I wanted to be – don't laugh. You used to say I had the face for it, or were you lying about that now too? – And not like Liam Neeson or Colin Farrell the langer – more sort of a, sort of a Gabriel Byrne sort a actor – did you know he was a teacher for a while? Yeah: for kids like. He was just a regular guy.

You see me if you don't know me and you think I must be some kind of breathing dead who just lives to drive drunk suburban sociology majors back up Barracks Hill, or get pissed with his mates on Friday night and beat the shite out of pissers from Limerick – but I want more than that, Anne. That's what I'm on about here. Your man Macbeth, he's just frustrated. Misdirected, misunderstood. And I feel that in me, that desire he has to be somebody, to kill if you have to, to get somewhere. *(Pause.)*

Jesus, Anne. This place is a dump. Smells like beer and piss. You'll never get anywhere directing plays here. *(Pause.)*

– Right so:

I've memorized it. I know I didn't have to, but it's his first –
soliloquy, and I'm going to do it for you. Okay? Jesus … This is like
mortally terrifying. – And now don't you be doing me no favors on
account a we used to go together. Don't be nice to me on account a you
like me as a friend and because we have a "history" together – a recent
history. I'm nobody, okay? I'm a stranger. *(Pause.)*

   – Can I ask?

   Is it true you're moving to London?
   For good?
   Is he going with you? *(Silence.)*
   Right so. Fair play. I'll start:

   This supernatural soliciting
   Cannot be ill, cannot be good. If ill,
   Why hath it given me earnest of success,
   Commencing in a truth? I am Thane of Cawdor –

   Fuck.
   Can I start again?
   – Can I try something here?

   (Begins shadow-boxing again.)

   This supernatural soliciting
   Cannot be ill, cannot be good. If ill,
   Why hath it given me earnest of success,
   Commencing in a truth? I am Thane of Cawdor.
   If good, why do I yield to that suggestion
   Whose horrid image doth unfix my hair

And make my seated heart knock at its ribs

Against the use of nature? Present fears

Are less than horrible imaginings.

My thought, whose murder yet is but fantastical,

Shakes so my single state of man that function

Is smothered in surmise and nothing is

But what is not.

(Stops boxing

Breathes.)

I did it better on my own. I did it in front of a mirror, just saying it like it was regular words like. – And I hope you don't mind me boxing, but I feel like he's boxing, like he's hopping from side to side, trying to figure out what to do, what's real. He's fighting his own shadow, know what I mean like? – You never really saw that in me, did you Anne? I mean, you just thought I was one sort of man and Des was another, and you chose him because he had complexity and sophistication and "art." But you see, all personal taste aside Anne, we've all got "art" in us, it's there, we just don't know how to *say* it all the time, or we don't want to say it all the time, but we all have "feelings." – All I'm saying is, you never knew the real me. You never gave me half a chance, and I know you still love me, Anne – you do, but you're scared I'm nothing. – But see, that's not me. That nothing part's not me. I'm someone. I'm going to be someone. I'm going to go somewhere. You think I won't be famous and I won't be able to give you money. You think you're all progressive and women's liberation and shite but you really want to live quite comfortably now don't you, Anne? You want to be taken care of. – And I can do that for you! Maybe not now. Maybe I'm young, and I don't know what my calling in life is yet, maybe I don't have a fucking clue about anything and I'm destined to do nothing but sit here and eat and drink and fuck on the odd old night, but I love you, Anne, I want you, I got you in my fucking blood and I can't get you out of it …

My heart's always pointing in your direction. No matter where you go. *(Silence.)*

Right.

Right so.

I didn't mean to frighten you. I know there are other people waiting – . *(Silence.)*

– I want to take your little man Des outside and run him over so his bones are breaking like a symphony beneath my tires. I want to stick my hand down his wee throat and pull out his beating black heart and throw it in the God damned River Lee. – But I'm not going to touch him. I'm not that kind of man. You've got me so I don't even know who I am. *(Pause.)*

Can I try it again? the soliloquy?

You're a brilliant girl – you're a woman – I could listen to you talk all night. Your ideas, your talent – Jesus! it's like God fucked up drowned you in talent! When I saw you doing that play, what was it, before Christmas – in this room – you were so alive I thought if I could just find a way to fit my hands round your ribcage I'd feel your heart beating in there like a bird inside a drum …

– What do you mean I don't know you? *(Pause.)*

Right so. I'm going. *(He takes a folded piece of paper out of his sock.)*

I wrote this poem for you. *(Unfolds it to read; reconsiders. He drops it on the floor.)*

You can read it on your own time. It's not fucking Shakespeare.

– And while you're at it: Forget what I said. Forget I even auditioned. And don't even think about casting me, I wouldn't take the part – .

(Blackout.)

East

(Dublin. Late night. A man sits drinking sherry.

A tape cassette of monks chanting:)

PETER

I think you should remain right where you are. Here, in Dublin.
That's what I think. Why? Because this isn't America. We care about
our writers here. We care about the theatre, as a living, breathing
body of work. There's a different mindset here. In my opinion. Get
away from everything you've ever known, everyone you've ever been,
and you may find that you see things with clarity, finally.

Sherry?

Friends gave this to me, for my birthday, it's French. It's
wonderful: dull, tangy taste, like death. That was a joke. I imagine
death is dull – but tangy? No … Yes! this liquor, this music … reminds
me of a monastery I once visited in Brittany. Have you been? to
France? Oh you must. I'd been walking for days, alone, through the
countryside. All I had was some water in a bottle and my compass,
pointing north, always due north because I knew that I had to find the
coast. I needed to find the coast. And when I found the coast, which
was quite desolate, rocky – Celtic, really – I heard voices coming from
inside a small stone hut. A stone church. Music like the stones were
singing …

I stayed for three weeks. The monks gave me a room, fed me.
No one ever said a word to me. *(A very long silence.)*

You should try it, this sort of silence. You should go to the
continent. Go east, young man! Istanbul, Lithuania. Go where
you don't know the language – it's liberating when a writer doesn't
know how to speak. When the language is babble. An equilibrium
is achieved between the landscape inside one's own mind and the

landscape without. That's the one danger as a writer, drowning in yourself. *(Pause.)*

How do you find Ireland?

Do you think the Irish are the soul of literature? I do.

It's rather mystic, isn't it? First time I came to Dublin, for one of my plays, my mother was convinced I'd be shot, or hijacked or car-bombed or what have you. It didn't matter how much you explained that No Mum, the bombing's in Belfast. To the English, Ireland means violence, savagery – animism. – There's some truth in that though, isn't there? The rocks here sing … Something ancient here. Primal and life-loving here …

Wouldn't you say? *(Silence.)*

You remind me of myself at your age. I hope you don't mind me saying.

Are you going to France? I have some friends still in Lyon. – When I was your age I lived on an island off the coast of France for some time. I'd been acting for years. I woke up one morning and said to myself, Sod it Peter, do it now or you're never going to! So I left everything I knew, and I went to France and bought a loaf of bread on the mainland and took a rowboat out to my new home. Lived there for seven and a half months. – When I came back I had a beard and spoke French with my first play under my arm, which was picked up right away. That's the only time I've worked without a commission. I enjoy commissions very much, don't you? I'll give you some numbers to ring in Lyon. *(Silence. He picks up a sheaf of papers.)*

Would you like to hear something new?

It's about Princess Di. It's a dark comedy.

The scene is Buckingham Palace. The young Princess has just discovered that Charles has been carrying on an affair with Camilla what's-her-name:

"Charles, I can't believe this! We're husband and wife."

Charles: "No dear, we're a royal marriage – there's a difference."

Diana: "You can't sleep around with whomever you like, Charles!"

Charles: "And can't I? And why not? – I'm to be King one day!"

Diana: "Because it's immoral, Charles! Adultery is immoral! What will the children think?

Charles: "The children will never know."

Diana – bursting into tears: "They will! They will! The Children always know!"

Charles: "There there, Di. There there, 'presh. Don't cry. Why don't you go shopping with Fergie?"

– "I hate you! I hate you so damned much, Charles! I'm going to go out and have affairs of my own!" She cries. *(Pause. Composing himself.)*

– Just more of the same, really.

How's your glass? Would you like another? *(Silence.)*

Quite a babe, wasn't she? Diana? Rest in peace, old girl …

I find it fascinating the level of grief her death inspired. The veneration of this poor woman. It all seemed quite selfish. I think the only reason we keep the monarchy intact is for mytho-psychological reasons, by which I mean we need a Queen, we need Princes and Princesses, to stand for that part of ourselves that wishes to possess power and virtue. And of course these people can never *be* that, because none of us are all-powerful, all-virtuous, or at least not all of the time – and that's what gives you drama! Set up an unreal expectation of a person, then watch it inevitably, inexorably, ineluctably crumble. It's very dramatic that, very Greek. *(Pause.)*

Well.

Why don't you tell me something about your writing: *(Silence.)*

Um-hmm. *(Silence.)*

Um-hmm-mm. *(Silence.)*

– Now *that's* very good, isn't it?

Here's what I think. And I know I've just met you, but I meet young writers all the time and you seem to have something. – There's something *in* you, isn't there? You talk a lot, but it's bubbles on top of boiling water – there's something *deeper* in you. Isn't there. I think, if you leave America, if you stay here in Dublin – get away from anything you feel you know – you'll discover who you truly are. It's very difficult for young writers to discover who they truly are. *(A hesitation:)*

Will you be writing in ten years?

Are you so sure … ? *(Slight pause.)*

Don't be offended: you're young. Writing is hard work. The writer's life is hard. It's constant suffering. It's a love of constant suffering. The impulse to write is not enough. The poetic propensity – the disability – *that* is not enough. – Are you haunted? may I ask? Have you ever been suicidal? Do you have secrets you know you'll take with you to the grave? – You see, there's such a romantic notion of what a writer does, when in fact it's just lonely, lonely-making work – the best work borderline psychotics can find, and once in a very odd while you find another hopelessly charming American at your door who wants you to sign another copy of your latest God damned bloody play! *(Pause.)*

You see? – what I'm saying? *(Pause.)*

I don't talk to people … I don't like people … I'm sorry if I'm disappointing you in some way. *(Silence.)*

… This place used to be a pen factory. Did you know that? I like that fact. They turned it into studios for artists. You can hear the jewelry maker shuffling overhead, the painter next door scratching her canvas with her bristles. No one ever speaks to you. Do you mind if I kiss you? *(Silence.)*

– I'm not gay either.

I was gay, for a while, but it really wasn't me. – I don't want to fuck you. *(Silence.)*

Can I hold your hand then? *(Pause.)*

… You have strong hands. These hands make things. And your eyes. You remind me so much of myself at your age. When I opened the door and saw you standing there all wet from the rain … I thought, I really must take him in. Really must take care of him. *(Stands abruptly:)*

No, don't apologize.

– I'm sorry, I'm sorry. Have I – ? I hope I haven't spoiled anything – .

Yes.

All right.

Good night. Yes it was lovely meeting you too.

(Blackout.)

West

(The west of Ireland. Music. Morning.
A woman at the door drinking from a coffee mug.)

MAEVE

Sagittarius. *(Pause.)* Am I right?

Quester, traveler, arrow-throwing centaur. *(She fires an imaginary arrow.)*

Aren't you – ?

Come in, come in: We've been expecting you. *(She laughs.)*

– That's not true. I've never seen you before. But people expect that sort of thing from me, the way I look: "Maeve, Voodoo Queen of Connacht." – Where from, pet: New Jersey? Westchester Country perhaps? All alone in the world this morning? If I murdered you would anyone notice you were gone? *(Slight pause.)*

I know, that's not very funny. But I say it all the time to visitors. *(The coffee:)* – Would you care for some? It's Irish Cream. Light on the cream, I'm afraid. *(She revolves.)*

– Welcome to Bally Phallus, wayfarer! Or Castle Clare, as it's known among the indigenous. More a Leaning Tower of Limerick than anything remotely Arthurian – and not a very well-endowed phallus, if you ask me, as you might well have noticed but you'll see. On a clear fine day you can see all four corners of the earth, or Ireland at least. – Shall we? *(She climbs a step:)*

The box on the table is for the five pounds Irish suggested donation. – Or you can pay in weed, if you'd rather. If you have any. *(Another step:)*

Do you have any?

– Oh, you're definitely a Sag'. My son's a Sag'. You can always tell with a Sagittarius just what it is they're thinking of you. *(She revolves; a room; she picks a book off the wall:)*

These are my husband's books. It's pornography. "Erotica." The whole library's full of it. Burt – my husband – he's an avid collector of rare and often ancient erotica. He's got too much money. And a predilection for young girls. And once even a young man though I can't quite prove it yet. But don't worry: he's in Montreal. We have a house there.

Why do men like pictures so much?

This particular volume of pornographic etchings is over three hundred years old – and French. Of course. It's not very good pornography, if you ask me – can't make out any of the *parts*, but that's why it's called erotica, isn't it? I don't care. Keeps me warm at night, which is important for a woman in her prime … What did you say your name was? *(Silence.)*

And you need a place to stay?

How did you hear about us out here?

– Come, come: talk and walk. *(She climbs.)*

Um-hmm. *(Silence.)*

Um-hmm-mm. *(Silence.)*

You flew in this morning? You must be positively dizzy – .

Watch your – ! They made these steps of unequal height in order to trip the assassins who might come at night to murder the king or the clan chief or the grand poo-bah what-have-you. It's true. – Now duck your head, sweet thing. You have an honest face. Your aura – . You're making me happy this morning. *(Revolves.)*

This is my son's room.

The kids sleep here now. – Not my kids – I don't have any besides James – "the kids" are what I call my pupils. They come in all ages. From all over the world. They're coming this weekend. We host conferences here at Castle Clare. We sleep on the floor, on mats. "Unlock Your Psychic Potential" – that's my calling in life. Don't worry, no one's serving Kool-Aid. We're a nexus, a way station, we don't care for science-fiction or comets. People come here of their own accord and they don't know why, they're following a magnetic current, if you will, an attraction even they don't understand. But they've wandered, and they've suffered, and they've come here to get healed. – And you came.

Why?

Why did you come, of all places, to Ireland? Because something called you. Something drew you to us – . *(Revolves; she stretches out her hand; shivers.)*

Oh … *(Slight pause.)*

You have something in you, don't you?

Is there someone with a "C" in your life … ? *(Silence.)*

Is she alive? *(Silence.)*

And you're still in love with her? *(Pause.)*

Well you know what Yeats said – .

When my son died, I was distraught. I thought: Life is over for me now. – Everyone thinks that when they're in pain. When you're in pain, there's nobody else, is there? The world is full of people, an infinite number of people, an infinite grief. – What makes you so special? My boy hung himself in this room. You wouldn't know it by looking at me. And still I don't know why.

But then one night, long after, I heard him speak to me. Right over my shoulder, like he was in the room with me, he whispered, "Mom, won't you answer the door for me?"

And so I've been answering the door, ever since, no matter who knocks. You are evidence of that. *(Slight pause.)*

– Where are you going?

– We haven't finished the tour yet – *(she shivers violently:)*

– Stop it! Wait – hold everything!

James is here. My son. He wants to say something: – What is it, darling? Yes, dear. I know. – He says he thinks maybe you should stay. Help me get this place in order, so that my students have somewhere nice and tidy to sleep when they arrive. – I know, James. I know I need help. I can't do it all on my own. – He's is a very forceful male. Like his father that way. – I hear you, James dear, but he doesn't want to stay! I'm afraid I've scared him away! He has places to go, all of Ireland to see. He's a young American wanderer. We can't keep him here forever, can we?

… Oh, James.

… That's a good idea.

… Yes, James, I'll tell him. Good-bye. *(She kisses her hand.)*

– Stay. For just an hour or two.

Take a nap. The bed's already made for you. We can finish the tour in the evening, which will be morning for you. *(Pause.)*

Of course you're tired. You're broken hearted. *(Pause.)*

Of course … the journey … *(She holds out her arms.)*

Come here: You're home for now.

(Lights rise. Then blackout.)

Am Lit,

or

Hibernophilia

JOE

Kate.

Remember me?

It's Joe.

I remembered you today. Going through some old box and
what should I find but you? – a picture of you – you and me in Cobh.
"Site of sinking of the Lusitania." An Italian tourist took it. That
statue of the emigrants leaving Ireland behind, pointing out across
the ocean toward New York. In the picture I have my right nostril
hooked onto the pointing, sculpted finger of a famine victim. You are
laughing gorgeously.

What is it about that country? Your country, I mean – Ireland.
All these years, I can't seem to get it out of my mind … I remember,
when I came home, with that accent and a scorching case of
mononucleosis – what was it? twenty-five, -six years ago? (Jesus Christ!
Jesus!) – and the nurse was taking blood and she could see I was about
to pass out from the sight of it, and she said:

"Do you think the Irish are the soul of literature?" (She knew
where I'd been.)

Well I couldn't answer, you see; I'd already passed out.

But the point is I think they are: I think you are: the soul of
something, for sure.

You will say I am being romantic. You always said I was
hopelessly that way.

– I can't believe I'm writing this.

I've wanted to write you a hundred times – thousands. But each time I got a page in I said, Now whom am I writing to?

Whom?

You know what I mean, Kate?

So how've you been?

Someone told me once that you got married, I forget who. Connor, I think. I saw him in Boston in the snow on a street corner years ago.

Do you see him much anymore?

I got married too.

And I'm writing because I've been thinking, Kate:

About Ireland, but not all that hokey stuff, the bogs and pints and dog shite on the sidewalk, but things like the weather, like walking through Cork City like a beehive with you in a misting warm rain, or the sweet burnt smell of hops and barley lying fat like fog in the gutter off South Main; or that moon in April when we drove all the way out to Blarney Castle because I'd told you – I'd told you I liked you and you said you liked me too and what else could we do but drive out into the country, and pull over in the weeds, and kiss, and talk, and make love, your face like touching a mirror – .

I swear I'm not being romantic. Not on purpose.

And I'm not drunk, either.

I don't write poetry anymore: I'm a college professor now.

And I'm writing you because I'm leaving, America, for good. I'm coming back to Ireland. And I would very much like to see you again, if you happen to be free.

***

Dear Genealogy Detectives:

I saw your ad in the *New Yorker*.

I am planning to return to my ancestral homeland of Ireland soon, and would very much like my roots dug up for me.

Here is what I have already:

My father's family starts with three brothers who came to the U.S. from God knows where – Ireland, we think – and two of the three died in the American Civil War.

Union-side. There's no proof whatsoever anyone ever lived down south, thank God.

So anyway:

My grandmother's mother was from the Alsaice-Lorraine region of France, which might make her French or German, depending on the dates.

Her mother was married in Wexford, so there's Viking blood in me, no?

Her father came from England, I'm sad to say.

– But here's an interesting story:

This side of the family is descended from a famous English poet who wrote satirical verse concerning rich people with flatulence.

Yes! It's true! To this day that poet has a plaque in Westminster Abbey. I shit you not.

His son lived in New York following the American Revolution and knew Ben Franklin – who was quite flatulent, by most accounts.

His great-grandson (my great-grandfather) was the vaudeville comic who wrote the famous "Talking Horse" sketch of 1896, which was subsequently stolen from him and bastardized in that 1950s television show, the title of which I refuse to mention.

"A horse is a horse of course of course … "

To all inexpert calculations that makes me 5/8 Irish, 1/8 Franco-Prussian, and 1/4 English. But you can make statistics say just about anything, so – .

Some other facts you might find helpful whilst digging: I am of above-average height. My hair is thick and silver-tinged. I am newly widowed, a professor of American Literature at a small midwestern liberal arts college that shall remain nameless. I have been told I have what is sometimes referred to as a "Mid-Atlantic" accent, but I think that's only because I make a point of speaking correctly. I have a vaguely Semitic nose, but that could be more nurture than nature (too long a story to explain here). A tarot card reader once told me I was destined for a great journey, but be careful, she said, "You have eyes that suggest a susceptibility to magic."

– What do you make of all that?

I know it's confusing and I can't guarantee the "truth" of anything I've just written, but I will treasure tremendously anything you can find about who I really am, genealogically speaking. Money is no object. Just send the bill, or perhaps I will pay in person next time I'm in Dublin.

***

Con:

Long time no email.

Hope you haven't given up your Socialism. Hope you haven't bought a tooth to plug that charming gap of yours. "Teeth are so bourgeois!" (Sideways smiley face.)

Remember that? "Line up all the landlords and have them shot." Aha ha – (Sideways winkie smiley face.)

Good craic, good craic.

Remember the pub with the ghost of the dead monk in it? What was it called? *The Well?*

I don't remember when last we spoke. Probably, what, that day in Boston when you were in town for the Poli Sci? And you mentioned Kate. Might you happen to know if she's still hitched?

Anyway, I'm writing because I'm leaving America. For good. And I'm wondering if there might be a teaching position you know of somewhere in your country? If you're still at this e-address, you're still in Galway, and if you could poke around for me, I'd be much obliged.

Do you know where I've been?

Nowhere. Smack dab in the middle of Middle America. That is, Heartland.

It's been terrifying.

I've always been terrified of America. I've tried to be patriotic, to get hot for flags and eagles and guns and FreedomLibertyHappiness for all and all that other bullshit, but to quote your friend Mr. Joyce: "I distrust those big words which make us so happy." And he was talking about patriotism too.

Of course there's always the possibility I'm a snob.

I remember arguing with you, years back. You were of the opinion, still quite popular, that Americans have no real culture. Certainly white America doesn't. And that by extension American Literature, you said, has the aesthetic weight of a quilt.

I forget what my defense was. Something about rugged prose: Huckleberry Finn and Hemingway.

Well you know what? After all these years:

I think Henry James is just about the most boring thing I've ever read.

And Mark Twain? Racist. Hemingway? Self-hating gay.

Leatherstocking Tales? Don't even get me started!

(Dickinson I like; but you know how much I love women.)

And it's not just the books! American students are hopeless. They come to class and can't finish a novel. Can't construct a full sentence. Can't read. Even those that are semi-literate have no idea how to *really* read. They watch the movies of the books I assign. Do you know how difficult it is to find classics of American Literature that do not have cinematic corollaries?

Everyone's so obsessed with being fem lit or gay lit or black lit or even dead white lit for that matter because they have no idea who they really are!

But the Irish know exactly who they are.

You will say this is just Joe being romantic again.

You will say the Irish are no more cultured than Americans.

People kill people in Ireland too, you'll say. (Let's not talk of Belfast, Con. Belfast's not Ireland, and we both know it.)

I read somewhere that Limerick is called "Stab City": a man attacks a crowd with a knife and he does relatively little damage; give that man an automatic handgun however – .

But no! the Irish are kind and hospitable!

The Irish are poetic, and musical.

The Irish have lovely lilting tongues.

The Irish are stubborn, yes, but – .

The Irish are passionate dreamers!

The Irish are a race of children.

The Irish know the world of myth and mystery.

The Irish are entertaining liars.

The Irish are sentimental.

The Irish are drinkers, yes of course, we confess; they stay up late evenings writing old friends desperate emails if you don't get me this job Con I'm going to fucking blow my brains out.

(Sideways winkie smiley face.)

Ha ha, got you there, Con!

What do you say?

Reply A-SAP, and let me know:

I can teach anything: Yeats or Synge or Wilde or Joyce or Beckett, or Synge – Edna O'Brien! – or Shaw or Keene or Behan or Friel doesn't matter just somebody who's not American for fuck's sake Con please – !

***

Hello?

Hi – who's this?

This is Joe. Who's this?

– *Who's* this?

Oh, Aunt Josephine – I didn't recognize – . Why are you there?

Yes, well I'm out in –

Yes well it's hard to get away from –

Listen – can I speak to Mom?

Sure, I'll hold.

(Jesus H. –)

Hello?

Yes Aunt Jo; still here.

Yes I got your card.

Yes it's a year now. One year exactly this week.

Hard to believe.

Thank you.

Thank you so much.

– Comedic, I think.

I said it's not "tragic" really, it's "comic." Tragedy implies my wife was somehow guilty of something.

I said tragedy implies – . Oh forget it.

– Can you please put Mom on?

...

Hi Mom, it's Joe.

No, I'm not the mailman.

No I'm not John your nurse, I'm –

Your son.

Listen, I wanted to let you know that I'm moving and –

To Ireland.

I know you're Irish. Your maiden name was – I know all that. I remember.

The real reason I'm calling, Mom, is I could use a little help.

Just for the transition, really.

After that, I'll be able to save again ...

What do you think? Can you help?

... Well that's a fantastic dish, isn't it.

Who? And Barbara doesn't mind. I said your friend Barbara doesn't mind that he's sleeping with – . Oh he's not. Well that happens when you're older. Yes I agree physical love is an integral part of a healthy relationship – .

Margaret was killed, Mom. In a movie theater, in the afternoon. A man walked in near the end of the movie and shot sixteen people, then shot himself ... He kept saying, "Do you know who I am?"

Mom?

No no, I already spoke to Aunt Josephine – .

***

Mrs. George Boyle (neé Katherine O'Sullivan), #10 Lockview
Drive, Clashduv, County Cork, IRELAND:

Dear Joe,

[My God, her handwriting!]

I got your letter today by post ["by post"!] forwarded to me
by my mother who is still alive if you'll believe it now and was v.
surprised and I read it three or four X over and still can't make heads
nor tails of it but am writing you back all same and thought I'd better
send it quick.

[She never understood commas, what is it with women and
commas?]

Were you lit when you wrote it? You seemed right pissed,
[comma, thank you] listen I'm flattered you're thinking of me but I
don't think it's deserved I'm at least 47 now and you should see my
arse in spandex I'm still happily married thanks.

[Shit.]

I have 8 children.

All of whom are doing well Ryall's in university and Sinead runs
a dot-com if you can believe it now that does the research for lineage
for the Americans with nothing better to spend their money on.

[Shit shit.]

And I'm sorry to say but your [sic] mistaken in your [sic]
memory of that night at Blarney Castle because I've never been to
Blarney with you or anyone else [commas, woman, commas!] though
you and I once snogged in a parking lot behind *The Blarney Stone* a pub
in Ballincollig it's true! I remember it was v. cold in the car and I did
not enjoy it one bit our kissing nothing personal you were not my type
don't you wonder why we never kissed again?

[…]

At this point I think it's safe to say we hardly know each other, don't you – ?

***

Hey.

    (Hey.)

    What's up?

    (Nothing.)

    How's school?

    (Fine.)

    Listen: We should talk. Sit down. No really. – You know how I used to live in Ireland –

    (No.)

    Well I did. Twenty-six years ago –

    (You never told me that.)

    Well I – I actually have told you that. I'm sure I have.

    (No. I don't think so.)

    The point is I've been doing lots of thinking, since your mother –

    (snorts)

    – Since your mother – . And I've decided to move back.

    (– ?)

    To Ireland.

    (You fucking kidding me?)

    Just for a while. Not for good. For a year maybe – we'll play it by ear –

    (I'm not going.)

    You have to. You're my son.

(I'm not going – !)

Look, I know this is a lot to handle –

(Why don't you ask me? Why don't you *ever* talk to me?)

I'm talking: I'm talking to you right now: Talk to me:

(… This is – I don't – God! – Whatever!)

Listen, I understand how you feel –

(– Bullshit! You don't understand shit!)

This is not a big deal, James! It's like getting a job transfer, and would you please lower you –

(What am I supposed to do in Ireland? Hang around with a bunch of fucking leprechauns?)

They're not leprechauns, James – they speak English – and since when is it okay to swear at your father?

(Sorry, guess I'm just speaking fucking Irish now!)

This is not open to debate! We are moving to Ireland and that's – !

(What's so great about Ireland?)

It's where you're from – it's who you are – don't you want to know who you are?

…

Fine. We can figure out a way for you to stay here. With friends or something. Until I come back.

***

Dear God,

No one seems to think this is a very good idea.

I wonder if you could make things a little clearer for me.

Because it made perfect sense a couple weeks ago.

But now I'm doing all sorts of weird things.

Like praying.

I don't even know if I believe in God.

– Isn't that funny?

But my faith, or lack thereof, doesn't even seem like a question I should answer right now.

You'd think, after everything I've been through this year, that I'd want to know for sure that there was someone on the other end of this line, listening.

I know there's someone listening.

But what I really want, as long as we're talking wishes, is to be able to talk to her …

Please God protect me on my journey. Keep my son safe here with his Aunt Josephine, may he forgive his poor foolish father this, his heart's whim.

Amen.

(Is that my cell phone ringing?)

***

JFK International Airport, eight-hour layover, halfway home (to Ireland).

Dear Diary:

There's something about New York.

I am sitting now in the Pizza Hut kiosk.

There are fat people everywhere.

So many different races of fat people.

Not in Kansas anymore.

People are saying the strangest things to each other.

It's remarkable really.

I'm catching pieces of it, just fragments really.

"Do you know where all the shoes stores are at?"

"Do you know in certain folk loric tales – ?"

"No no I can't why don't *you* get a job and help *me*?"

"Shut up baby you want fifty cents right now?"

You know they're just places people go to get hookers and coke.

Can I get a large hazelnut?

Can I get a whoop whoop?

Can I have a *(gesture)* flat top?

(gesture) *(whispers)* O.K.

You welshin me?

You jappin me out – ?

Don't you jew me – !

Excuse me, sir, are you Italian?

No.

What is the word, I can't think of that word in Italian –

I'm sorry. I can't help you –

Give me the mirror.

I don't know where it is.

Give me the fucking mirror!

I told you I haven't seen it – !

You can't get a real slice today anywhere.

How modern …

Waat?

How modern!

I fear those big words which make us so happy.

I just want to know where it is.

I just need to know where I left it.

THE CHAMELEON

A WOMAN

Can a woman disappear? when her children have grown her
beauty her body gone When she's old too old to look at blent into
background a ghost in the fog Do you think a woman can get lost
Do you believe in that or is it psychology I mean how do we know
it's different than say religion which I've never much cared for I was
Episcopal on Sundays as you know then holidays less so as I aged
what do you think of Freud? do you think he was correct? I took a
novel course two months in college where the trees were penises and
girls in red dresses got periods Symbolically now what do you make
of that? do you believe in symbols? or is it just a matter of what we
see so it's something to us if we look at it long enough it's personal
for example why movies make me melancholy is my mother's fault
you see because when she lost it finally she took us out of school in
the daylight to watch films in the dark beside her she'd cry about her
husband my father and her son my insane brother all men everywhere
we couldn't see her crying but we heard.

> I loved school as a child.

> I loved to learn.

> I cried when I had to leave.

> It's not easy being a mother though so don't judge her
prematurely once you've tried it you'll see what I'm saying kids are
hard to mold the way you want to not doctors or lawyers or I don't
have a serial killer for a son thank God though there's one I've often
wondered about you know who he is why hasn't he even kissed a girl
he's shy it's the pornography if you ask me when he flunked out of
college I found pictures in his closet for God's sake pictures of Women
I won't have that in my house I said Disgusting pictures what if they
were your sisters your mother that shut him up quick all right all out

there all naked open to no mystery no mystery in that I never looked again to see he'd thrown them out he won't tell me anymore anything he's divorced his own mother at thirty-one -two -three years the age at which young men become Christ or rapists I've often wondered why so many things get wrecked by good intentions do you think I'm really that bad?

I wonder, inwardly.

It's difficult to be a mother, that's for sure.

You'd think some people are born for it!

I was, in a way that's all I wanted as a girl ambition was for children one day I married your father I was not yet pregnant though everyone assumed I was in those days we were so young so elopement upstate because my parents were divorcing in the papers I wanted it that way romantic in the leaves gold and crimson with your father a plumber he said he wanted children then more than fame or money my parents have I mentioned ah ha ha were hopeless and his were not much better dead in the chest like reptiles they had no hearts like chestnuts ticking termites we swore we'd get married love our children fix things better than we'd had them but do you think that's possible? like genetics I think we didn't have that Genetics as a kid if you had kids who turned out wrong it was your own damned fault the damned mother's God damned fault not even the father was never and cold as but mother was God shaper of flesh of mind if the child grew malformed is it then why is it your fault the mother did it to him that's what happened with my mother because I have a brother older than me named you never met him so named or hardly heard him named I'm sure he's locked away still up north eternally twelve years old and Mother felt she'd done it to him so I see her differently now.

I enjoy these late hours.

When the world's asleep.

I don't much sleep myself maybe an hour here or there a night and not at once like dogs or cats like Lizards do lizards sleep?

yes I am a lizard like with eyes wide catching night a saucer or satellite dish convex what do you call it don't like sleep though makes me tired do you think we get less so as we get less young? giddy for the grave I'm morbid do you think I'm old now because I feel immortal now this time of night I hate the daylight plagued by not just the usual like never time to wash the clothes this door is open time leaves in the most boring ways I'm left behind you see I'm saying I can't help but wonder what it is I've ever done wrong.

People die and people are born.

Thank goodness more people are born!

I read somewhere many places there's a river of time and we're in it from birth till death we carry along I read so much fiction nonfiction more not poetry because symbols don't like them much like I said I like a nice straightforward shot of mothers in wartime and bastard children no trash I swear but even the sex parts I like if you don't tell it's true stories I love most biographies of men who've lived and women it's not made up but what happened or might have happened to make things turn out this way or that Why a person makes this choice or that I believe in choice don't you not abortion or sex before marriage God no but what if there is no choice is something we tell ourselves while we're here in the mix of it Time the river and maybe it's all fated like evolution or inheritance at least if you're a mess then there's someone else to blame.

In the day I feel my brain age: clump of wet earth drying.

Mold sets.

At night I feel better running water like a like a what like a what exactly?

I have a metaphorical mind It's true like a Like always fond of saying similes once I was told in night school if I were not a mother I would be a Laterally Thinking Academic a novelist or journalist at least wholly unlike your father who didn't want me in school even when all of you were gone he thought I'd meet a man for God's

sake at my age my state I'm stout beyond shapely jealous he was
not college educated a Plumber before all else last week my bladder
slipped partway out it poked through snail out its shell groundhog
saw its shadow ah ha ha I've got a morbid sense of the what the
absurd to think I'd have an affair never having seen a man but your
father and your brother's pictures do women really want that I've
often wondered I mean I've wanted sex I want it still like a deep like a
what for I'm not ashamed of nature dear I'll never understand a girl's
embarrassment wet and watery Christ people are a mess intellectually
I read somewhere many places men come in shapes and Do you
think that's true? glorious multitudinous well never mind it's late now
I'm interested in those things I want to see before it's gone what is it
what is the root cause of our situation here listen to me I have a high
I.Q. I'm not going to say the number now it's rude but my teacher a
womanish man walks up my front stoop I was a girl then says to my
parents on the screened-in porch they were drinking scotch a sunny
Sunday Congratulations your daughter is a genius! and they screamed
out laughter Ah ha ha Ah ha ha how how absurd they thought that
I should be a genius they skipped me a grade but no genius school
I'm afraid because I'd get married which was fine by me and what
did I know then what did they care when they were damaged goods
too as your father would say but he was jealous that my father the
businessman opened China making millions of clean white shirts
with slave labor tan hands and my mother dying her brown hair gold
could have been a movie star Sad she never said much but drank once
when she tried to leave the house mostly naked in a mink and bra and
panties after lunch I stopped her at the door and she beat and kicked
and scratched my face to get the eyes so I wouldn't ever see her again.

But you know all this. Don't you? I've told you all this before.

You are such a good listener. That's your talent.

I'm proud of you, especially you, do I tell you?

When you were a child you had pneumonia two times in one
year the last time I stood over you as you slept or tried to anyway

counting the breaths you took one two three for the doctor to know
how you were going to survive I stood I stood over you counting out
and in out and in until you were my child again.

It's been a long time since I saw you Not that I've missed
you or been I don't know inconsolable how time flies in this place is
so much more what than anywhere else I've known before what do
you think of that the idea that time passes our bodies change but
everything everywhere matter stays much the same Now the always
you're living Now speaking you're hearing me talk to You Now.

What do you think?

Does time pass? And where on earth does it go?

I think of these things, and my heart dries up.

But at night, I breathe, because nighttime is Don't you
think it's frightening if you're out alone in it as a girl I recall the fog
following me in autumn or winter wrapt round me like a fever I'd ride
my bike into white at dusk along country white sky skin the same I
could not see my arm's length ahead tempting fate listening for cars
the chuff and stampede of deer bodies rumbling dogs barking horses
magisterial cries high in the somber fog cries aloud in passion panic
If I lost the road I slid and bumbled through wet field and mud grass
blades slashing pants wet legs slithering down to rest I dreamed I'd
come out a new place and time but then night fell and the fog at night
is more beautiful because nighttime is daytime without light so why
are we scared the animal gets haunted can't help it at night animals
haunted by the absence of light where there once was our house is
empty I suppose a young family lives there and I pretend it's empty
still and haunt it in my reach my mind and walk there from room to
looking out on woods where your brother took his life Street where
your father opened his car door home from work when he worked
Oh countless times for me Oh life wrapt up in my arms you lumps
of clay Oh happy children I'm sure life was not all that bad was it
but equal parts my house full of Child empty now like a womb child
haunted I was always the wax or wane born to mother in my guts my

talent genes I went to a shrink not long ago who said I was simply
Sad adjusting to Sad the transition to It's hard she said Your problem
is you don't know who you are! and I said that's crazy insane no and
she fed me some feminist Who says I'm not strong had a hundred
and one children one man don't think I said much about him though
I should have to get my money's worth that's when she says You're
water look to others like a river mirror Chameleon for your color I say
a lizard a Chameleon it's a metaphor and I say I'm not stupid I began
to cry you know just a little in my eyes and she says Even now you're
giving me what you think it is I want to hear and see and I said that's
because I am nice.

      But maybe she had a point?

      What do you think, is she right? You decide.

      Can you spend your life disappearing in the act of it the fact
is the highest form of Christ got blent into the cross did I do more
harm than Tell me you turned out fine you of all did most everything
my way good boy good son sick I nursed you back to counting health
with my health breathing into you as if I could Perfect I wish to see
you now tell me why did everyone else go away what is it tell me
why I can't see you is it something I cannot name carried down in
repeated in the unto the third or fourth what do you call them tell me
I'll learn if it is my fault I'll open my come find my stay live with me
stay out of love you can't see come find me I promise I'll never hurt
you or take you or deny where are you I can't see you now come find
me again please

MIDNIGHT RADIO

VOICE

Are you there?

> Are you listening?

> This thing on?

> Listen, now; those things you're hearing? They're not true.

Or they might be true, you just don't know; those things you're hearing are just your head. Inside it.

> Nowhere else.

> Inside is strange; a mysterious – you have a very active mind …

> What is it – tell me – you think you're thinking?

> What is it you think you're hearing now?

> What do you think is happening to you?

> Who cares what I think; what do *you*?

> You don't know, do you … Poor boy …

> You're just a boy; you shouldn't be up this late …

It's a comfort to you, I know; to know there are people like you, awake this far into the night …

> (Their eyeballs disappear; their eyeballs turn to glue.)

> Some people are lonely, and some are sick.

> That's just how life is.

> Let me tell you what's happening:

> I'm older than your father is.

One day you'll find yourself in that small town where I am from, and you won't even know that you're there; that I'd been there, born there, grown up there, as they say; but you'll feel it in your bones.

Your bones grow while you sleep, you know.

They're meant to.

So sleep … or you'll remain a child forever …

You're a traveler; I know …

Let me tell you how it is:

What have you got against people?

What have you got against things?

What are you afraid of?

Microbes, the invisible divisible.

Your hands in hot water, gloves of frothing soap; the hot water makes the soap fall off, fall away into the drain down to the pipes down to the sea, away, imagined …

You can only imagine the sea …

You'll see the sea one day …

Have you? already?

I'm impressed.

– Where are your hands right now?

Show me:

Put them on your desk.

Your pillow, I meant.

You know what I'm saying: unlace them.

Who do you think you're praying to?

Why?

You've got demons, son: that's clear …

Inside. Your head.

Metaphorically speaking. They could be anywhere; this house, this body.

You know what that is?

A metaphor is:

True; and not true.

It is, and it's not.

It happened; yet not really … Not yet.

It is magic.

Everything you are afraid of has already occurred.

Think about it …

Let's consider this, then, the facts, shall we?

How many brothers and sisters do you have?

That many? That's too many …

And which one is it that sleeps inside your room? That one over there: is he older?

He's no good, is he? No. No use.

And how many parents?

That's a tricky question …

We all of us have two …

(Even I know that.)

I myself have no children, you see.

I wanted to but, you see – .

I'm older than your father, like I said. Your father is a boy in men's clothing.

I've had affairs – count them – of the heart; I was a free spirit ever since my youth, but mainly now I'm not.

No children that is except you. You're mine. All mine. All who are listening now …

You understand?

You see?

Don't you trust me implicitly?

You must not trust me *implicitly*. That was a trick question. Do you know who I am? from whence I speak? You imagine, I suspect, a small room in a dark building somewhere on the island of Manhattan. Not so far off.

(In the Garden there were two trees: two humans too.)

Let's get back to you:

Something is wrong in this house, in your head; and you do not know what it is.

You know, and do not know.

That's called metaphor.

Something in the family like a – . Like a what?

What's that noise? There.

Now, listen:

Hear it?

Someone is moving about inside the house after you all have gone to bed, to sleep; someone is awake at this hour of the night standing up there on the attic steps, or walking down the hallway, at the door to your – no: he's past now farther down still, down the hallway to the – someone has closed the bathroom door …

I think I know who that is …

But you tell me.

Because I know you know now too.

Look around: I'm not stupid, and neither are you. But you're in the dark, so to speak, on certain issues. And the sooner you learn the truth, the sooner we can get on with whatever it is we're meant to get on with.

The good work. Like this. My nighttime ministry.

You got it?

Now listen:

We're going to take a few callers here soon, maybe, if I feel like it, but – I'm from a family myself. A big one. And for the record I know what it's like to be small. Of the many unhappy multitudes.

Which is why I dedicate my life to what I do: language is first nature. A duck to water. My mother's tongue. It's like I'm no body these days, anymore. Ha ha. A mouth, a brain, and some voice some people find comforting, soothing. Some do not. Others are scared of me. I don't know why. It hurts my feelings. Some people do and others do not. It bothers me sometimes, to be so unpopular that I have to speak at night ... But how else could I be here with you?

You ought to be sleeping, you know; like children ...

Why?

Your bones grow while you sleep ... Like I said ...

What's keeping you awake? Let Daddy help you ...

It's your brother, I know: cat's out; the other one, who does not sleep in your room ... who sleeps above your head, in the attic.

He's the one you hear in the house. He's very ill, you know.

No one thinks so. No one speaks it: he's tried to murder someone. Did you know that? He threw himself out the window of his room in the attic over your head – and no one ever speaks of it. He tried to murder himself. But he's alive.

Not a bruise! Not one broken bone!

Angels caught him as he fell ... says your mother (who doesn't like church).

The trees, caught him as he fell ... The fanning branches of the snowy evergreen; the bed of snow ... (You skeptic. You're too young to believe.)

But how do you *know*?

But:

How do you know he fell at *all*?

That's right. You heard me:

How do you know something happened at all the way you think it happened?

You weren't there.

Remember: you're just a boy.

You did not see him fall. – You would have liked to have seen that: it would have been a riot. It would have left you mute. A saint. It might have made birds nest in your hands. It could have made your heart implode.

What you did see … was him walking up out of the trees, out from under the evergreens where he'd fallen. He fell. The snow was on his back …

But how do you know?

(You take it on faith.)

How do you know he took his own – *tried* to take it … ?

You don't: you were not there. You don't know. So shut up.

And murder is such a shame, the condition of wanting to murder one's own self, one's body, your mother has impelled you to shut up; and your father has kept quiet too, even unto you.

So say nothing too.

At school you're esteemed wise; chosen, older than your age. You are. A Hebrew king. Birds nesting in your hands.

But you're not.

Are you Old Testament or New?

Women your mother's age find you irresistible …

They confess this to you.

She held on to you that night.

After the angels, with your brother gone to the hospital; and your father – where was he? – She cried at the top of the attic stairs, Please don't tell anyone; she fell into your arms, and the music swelled. She sobbed in your arms and music swelled …

How peaceful you felt. How blessed.

... Your brother waits till you're asleep, now – he doesn't know you rarely sleep – then leaves his room and creeps downstairs, and creeps throughout the house all night ...

A ghost.

He's alive.

He's dead, and he is not ...

(He's a miracle, you know.)

He goes to the kitchen. He eats. Lots of sugar. A paperback book in hand. Fantasy ...

He watches TV.

Then upstairs to the bathroom. Where he remains for a very long time ... Mysterious.

What happens in that bathroom ... ?

Think hard.

He's sick in there. In some way.

He goes up to his room. He comes down. He goes up, comes down; up, down. – Is he sick? Is he coughing? Is that coughing or vomiting? Or nothing?

Get a grip, my boy. Get a hold of your self. If you don't hold on to your self you may find you have thrown yourself out the window yourself. You've got to rest. So your bones can grow. You will not grow if you're awake.

Do you have hobbies? for fun? Do you have fun?

Let's change the subject.

Of course you have fun ...

How all-American of you ...

Baseball: I see.

You want to be a second basemen when you grow up. Well – that's good. Peter was a second baseman. That's right: Saint Peter.

And Joseph played second base too – Christ's dad – or stepdad …
Paul was a utility player …

I'm joking, of course …

I blaspheme …

You won't be a baseball player; when you grow up. Sorry. I
know these things in advance. But dreams are good to have …

Baseball has beauty in it.

I'll grant you.

On a diamond, and the diamond full of light.

(The garden primeval; seraphim guard the gate.)

I prefer night games myself, because that's when I wake up.
But you:

You ought to play in the daylight, my boy, in the summer and
spring, the late, warming winter, sun-saturated day.

The light that fills the diamond …

Two trees in the garden, their fruits glisten in the sun …

… There – you fell asleep, my boy …

You did. You dozed. You see? Things aren't as bad as you
make them out to be … You hypocrite, you momma's boy.

I'm joking, of course.

Blaspheming again.

But it's true you think too much. You fear.

And fear corrodes: lets the danger in.

Don't fear or you'll have something to fear. I promise you.

Germs.

Including AIDS.

Cancers and all the inheritable diseases … (All that you know
of thus far.)

Insanity in all its variegated forms.

UFO abduction slash demonic possession (you haven't made up your mind yet on these two, have you).

– Remember you cried once you were convinced a syringe in the sand when you were ten or twelve (that long time ago!) had pricked you? – this has never happened by the way that you can recall; but how do you *know* it has *not* happened? how do you *know* it has not happened without you *knowing?* – and so you were certain you were dying …

You knew you would die soon. Your young life! You cried in the hallway at night outside your mother's door …

Ha ha. Ha ha ha …

I'm sorry, but it's funny to me somehow.

You'll appreciate this: you've got a philosophic mind. Soft, but inclined to grand distractions – I mean, assumptions – . So:

What do you think of the idea I have read that in the Garden there was one of everything – it's true: it was, and it was no metaphor yet. Yet as soon as we ate of that God damned fruit there were two. Of every single thing. In opposition: this and that. That like that. Or not. Metaphor and contraposition. Sickness and in health. Pain! Babel! Flood! Close-up: two seraphim guard the gates of Eden, like giant grotesque hummingbirds, no faces, their flaming swords (two) crossed above that flaming single gate. Vagina entrata. Ha ha. I know there was Adam *and* Eve, from the beginning, more or less, those *two* trees; you don't notice that at first. You don't *see.* When you found out, something split.

You see?

Do you see now what I'm after here tonight?

I'm trying to help you, you know …

You ought not to sleep with your fingers entwined … You ought not to pray so incessantly. (That means too much.) You talk too much too; God does not like that. He has other things to listen to. He abhors a chatter box. Christ did not talk like a house on fire, did he?

No, he made little sense. He alluded. He knew his audience (could not be trusted). He kept things hid. (And got crucified for it.) And he let his actions speak louder than – . He does not care how much you pray – God or Jesus: they told me so. And you ought not to sleep with your radio on like this beneath the pillow: it's bad for you; it can hurt your ears and head.

I feel sorry for you sometimes …

I do …

He's in the bathroom again, isn't he … ?

He's coughing; or he's vomiting. He's coughing. Vomiting.

He's sick. Not sick. You're not sick. You might be. Are you going to throw up … ?

There is nothing worse than throwing up in late winter …

I don't meant to make you sick by talking this way. Am I making you feel that way by talking this way?

Sometimes just thinking about sick can make you sick.

That's called being damned, either way.

(It's a metaphor.) (For what?)

What you fear has already occurred …

No, I'm not being facetious. Where'd you learn that word?

I remember one night you fell asleep in the evening in early winter in your day clothes and when you woke up well past midnight you were sick.

Remember that?

Remember how once you woke up sick?

Once, you woke up:

You were not sick; then you were.

Your brother fell from the sky in daylight; then he walked away …

Your brother tried to murder. Your own brother – . He did not die.

He got over it.

He's gone.

There there.

He's gone back upstairs. Back to bed.

He's fine – see? He wasn't sick. (He was.) It's all inside your head ... There's too much inside there! Useless! Like an attic full of old junk! He's upstairs again ... in his bedroom and he's closed his door. He's in his room now above your head. Forget him.

Everything's fine now ...

Everyone's all right.

You're a good boy, now ...

You mean well.

You're smart.

(You're not.)

(You're not very smart.)

You don't think enough, not well. – So think harder!

You don't know what tendentious means. Do you?

How old are you and you don't know that word?

Or that word?

I have a tendency to talk too much. Like you. Tendentious means biased. Like your mother. Unlike Christ. I'm a good talker. There's a difference. Between talking and doing. Now, writing is both doing and talking. It's a metaphor. You have dreams of literature. I know. You forget when you wake up, but – . You remember only the dreams about baseball, or girls, or the Garden. It's best for you that way. Well, you know how I feel about all that – but books!

A year or so and you'll make that leap: from Mickey Mantle's biography (written with Herb Gluck) to James Joyce. Stephen Hero: that's you one day soon. Not smart though, not really. What Ibsen was for Joyce (you cocky shit). This will blow your mind. You'll see. While all the other boys are outside drinking beer in the darkling woods, carousing and fingering girls, you'll have your canonical copy of Joyce spread openwide upon the bedroom floor. In the quiet house redolent of death. You'll hold your breath. And that's what makes you sing.

All this talk of Irishness. All this silly Irish feelingness. You'll like it because it's foreign. You'll think it's familiar; you'll *feel* it. But you won't *see*. You biteen of an illuminator; you monk fond of the coil and the curlicue, the enjambed line – rhyme, I meant to say. You remind one of Gerard Very Manley Hopkins. You remind one of Vonnegut. Say the teachers. Without talent. You are like. You are like …

You still there?

Salvation …

In Ireland: can you imagine us there together … ?

Oh yes, I'll be there with you.

Imagine, then, Ireland: it will free you … I promise …

The Angles peopled Angle land. The air, it peoples Eire land. The earth is peopled as flowers flower. Fruit. You are the gardener with the sheers. Your brother is the flower of your family's sin. Pluck it.

– Wake up!

Sin of what?

Did I frighten you? Ha ha.

It's called a touch of glossolalia. What we have. Or is it logorrhea? (It sends you to the bathroom anyway.) Joyce had it yes but more refined. Acute. Not latent. He knew too many words …

What were we talking about when you so rudely nodded off?

Oh yes.

We were talking about where you'll go …

Do you think you'll like it there?

Do you think you'll be happier there instead of here?

Do you think you'll ever get away?

Remember summer evenings … Magisterial purple skies …
Oh the quiet deadend street …

(That's a metaphor indeed: deadend. Deadened is the pun.
Not a good one; but a start. Too on-the-nose.)

You grew up on the deadened street beside a marsh you called
the woods.

Remember that girl what was her name? Christine? an
Irish girl. Pretty, she was older. One year ahead of you at school.
Untouchable.

You used to choose to go to bed early, just so you could lie
there and think of her … Dream of her … awake. You know what we
mean. What ever happened to her?

Where is she now?

I remember, let's see: Timmy Dorian, Robbie Collins, and the
girl you three fought for.

She was sitting on the swing, beneath the evergreen, bed of
pine needles beneath. Sweetly turning. Ceiling of green. She swung,
or swayed, because the branch bent and swayed as she swung, and we
pushed her far. Side to side. We talked, and talked. She listened: the
perfect. Rib of my. The ache you felt. Still feel.

You sly illuminator you …

You never talked to her.

Never really. Never tried.

There was something in you. Would disgust.

There *is* something in you, isn't there?

(What you fear has already occurred.)

Do you hear that now?

Above:

He's moving round again.

What's wrong with him?

He's awake still, like you. He cannot sleep.

You're similar.

You're twins.

Jesus to your James. James the brother of Jesus, as you know.

Which are you, do you suppose?

He's like you. – He is and he's not. – How? You're both so *sad*. Why do you think you both have that? It's a mystery to me ... He's moving across the floor now, your brother overhead. The serpent. Your family the menagerie. You among them. But your brother is the serpent.

He's given you real knowledge. At a price.

Why?

Why?

Why can't you just be happy?

I mean, doesn't that bother you at all? (It would bother me.) The world is full of happy men and women. It's a lie that says it's not. You will not be happy ever. Mickey Mantle is a happy man. He was. An alcoholic. (I lied.) America is *full* of bright sunfilled diamonds in the cornfields and all that other – rolling freight trains and swings of bats and the swaying swing cradling a summer girl through twilight –

You see?

What's *your* excuse?

– Cheer up!

Do you think it's possible we were born too sad?

Any of us. I speak of myself now too.

Do you believe in destiny? You Calvinist; you proto-Presbyterian ...

Do you imagine God wrote characters just to torture them to death?

(Yes.)

What kind of Creator is *that?*

(An artist.)

He loves you, and he doesn't.

(You know your parents love you …)

What's wrong?

Whatever could be wrong with you?

We've got to figure this out. Tonight. You and me; together.

We've got to.

Let's go.

I'll help you.

How?

… I think I have the answer.

It's an observation, but it's true …

I've heard some others say this about you, but: you *dwell*.

You think too much.

"Obsess" is the word. More than you'll ever know.

And it's a condition …

You ought to have been diagnosed. They have pills for that these days.

You are there, in conversation, and you're not.

You're here, and yet you're somewhere else. You are of two minds. Or more.

It's dangerous sometimes.

Girls don't like you; they're scared.

Or overly intrigued.

You have got to learn to let things go …

Unlace your hands now. There, quiet your mind …

Life is long and you are young.

Life is long and – I'm sorry for you. Really.

I feel such sorrow for you. I wish I could hold you.

– Get up!

I say unto you:

Take up your bed.

I know, I blaspheme. Forgive me, forgive me, pray for me –

He's moving around again …

From the bed across the floor … His footsteps in the floor, in the ceiling, above your room, your imagination. You hear. He's walking to the closet. He's walking over there. I would. You know what's over there too, the closet. You've found it there before. You've been bad. You don't know why you've done it but you do. You once found your mother's diaphragm in her nightstand drawer; your father's condoms, sex manuals with diagrams, in your father's nightstand drawer. Babies come from there. – Your brother has a closetful of magazines. All the usual, and a few not so. The low-budget, the seedier; these repelled you. But the others: you liked. Didn't you. Don't you. You like them. It's all right. It's natural. It's a shame. You don't want to but you did. Your heart beating, the hands tremulous – . That means to shake. Shake hands with yourself. That's a euphemism. And a sin, what you did; but sin is also nature … Why would God do that to himself? Why would He *do* that? It's not a sin if it's with a girl you love. If it is a girl and not a photograph of one. Photography is sinful by its nature. The reason the world is so. It was a girl or woman first. In a room somewhere, in Manhattan. A prostitute or drug addict; and that's not very sensual. It was a woman first. Before it was a picture. What if they enjoy it? Some of them do. It's called a perversion when you enjoy what's bad for you.

You're perverted too.

… All right, all right.

I forgive you.

You are forgiven.

You're in your penitent phase. (It won't last long.) Abstinence is mortifying. Try not to think of the girls. Try not to think of naked women. Try not to – think of your mother. Think of Christine Donovan in the swing in the tree beneath branches above the bed of orange pulp as she swung through the deforming light of twilight, summer …

Your brother is moving across the floor.

– *He* likes pornography. – *He's* never had a girl and I don't think he ever will. – Your father's said as much. He said he'll remain a bachelor all his days. He said just that one time. On the beach, full of sun and sand, climbing up a dune. You were watching for syringes. You never spoke. You hated your father. Your father said your brother will remain a bachelor all his days.

What did he *mean* by that?

You are not your brother …

You are his opposite.

Not a mirror no, a negative.

You're similar in some ways though.

Admit it.

Like your brother; but not.

You are him, and yourself. And that's a metaphor.

James was Jesus's brother. One died nailed to a tree. Another told the story.

What is it about you that makes you both susceptible? to darkness and dwelling and pornography?

You're going to get a girlfriend. You're going to get a life. You're going to stay haunted.

But him?

He's up there in the attic. Growing fat; bald. Speaking less. He's growing. Not his bones, his flesh. His mouth is disappearing. He's like a flower: a pale bloom: flower of the family's – . Does he even exist?

Could it be that nothing has happened to you at all?

Nothing has occurred.

If you were abused, you don't remember.

You would remember. If it happened. Something happened. No.

Nothing happened to you both. It's all inside your heads. You share a head, a house. Your mother said Don't tell, and your father said Nothing. You've never said a word. You've told the secret many times but you've never told the truth.

... Your father walked in the Garden in the deforming light of dusk, and you saw him through the trees, and you wept and hid your self ...

You saw him walk up out of the trees. Your brother now; not your father. You are like the father now and he is instead your Adam: your brother's back was covered then in snow. Imperfectly. A slate blue sweater he was wearing. A boy's – you see? This mania for detail, you do not have the mind: the black crow. The melting snow. Talismans and metaphor and rhyme; you sly illuminator you. Sun warm winter day. Too early now for baseball; soon ... Baseball is the opposite of that day. Crow, snow, tree, sky.

You ask him why. If you could.

Shh: you would.

You don't know it yet but you *should* ask him.

You think you understand because you hate your parents too ...

You hate where you come from.

It's a sin but there: you've hated where you've come from. Because you were hated by them first.

Your father's not a monster, your mother's fond of saying.

What is he then?

We're not *monsters*, she will say. And she will say:

You think you've had it rough ... (And her eyes go, and her face goes.) My family was a menagerie. My family was worse, she'll say. Her family *was* – . How? You don't know. Imagine. Her mother – . Her father – . In Manhattan. He never looked behind. Her brother was – . No one knows. He had no diagnosis. You've never seen him or met him. You've heard him, your mother's brother, but never seen. A voice. He called you once and said Do you like baseball?

This is why you believe in narrative …

And tragedy.

And absurd things.

(Belief is not faith but love.)

Your mother never speaks: she speaks nonstop. That's called tragicomedy.

Why can't you let her go?

Why can't you let them all go, she wants to know – get on with it?

Forgive, and forget (that's called irony).

Why can't you forget?

Forget.

It's gone on too long. Let go.

Don't listen.

Don't think.

Shut up.

And sleep.

Your brother might be up there fashioning a noose right this moment now. When your mother says Go get him for dinner, and you climb those steps to him, you knock on his door, and he doesn't answer you push it open and there he is by God dangling from a – his body – hanging from a – what? Hanging from – there's nothing strong enough to hang himself from. This rope is tied to nothing.

He could kill himself again. (What you fear has already occurred.)

Sometimes when you think you hear him opening the window. Removing the storm window. Climbing up and falling. Throwing himself again. You hear the monstrous − . Are you hearing things? Outside. Don't lose your mind now, boy. Are you losing it? Who are you? Your mind is a home, your face − . The soul is water. − Has someone broken in? Someone is inside, living there, you forgot when, he's walking around inside. Who is it?

We're not demons, your father and I …

He is the flower of your family's sin …

His sin engendered by sin, engenders more …

You are the gardener, somehow …

He fell through trees; he fell through branches. The evergreen broke his fall. The hands of angels in the muscular trees. Carried him to the ground and the snow met him like a miracle, it did not happen: it happened, and it did not.

You are absolved.

The mystery insolvable.

You are unloved; but you're not.

I'm here.

Be still and know that I am speaking …

Perhaps you ought not to go to church so much. Perhaps you ought not to go. Take it for what it's worth.

Do you think you're sick? Don't go mad. (You're going to need glasses − just like your brother; so much for baseball. Tough life.) Do you feel sick tonight? You still might. Do you think maybe you still might fall? It happens to the best of us, often at night. After the deformations of twilight. I spoke to her. I gave it to her. Your body is least defended against, after midnight and before the dawn. − In the day you're strong; you will perform. Because no one knows you're abstracted. You hide it. You are a leader among men. Girls like you and boys want to be you: smart, funny, and American in every way

– everything he is not. You're nice. Just, you like to think. A judge.
Everything. You sly archangel you. Birds in your hands. You will
yourself to be the opposite of him. You will yourself. Beget your self.
You cancel him out with your skill. Kill him, in a way, if you have to.
You have to. You are the sheers to the flower, the fruit – . He is not the
problem, he is the flower.

He hates you though. You know he hates every one of you.

He hates you, and he doesn't.

How do I know?

You misunderstand ...

I'm trying to explain.

I'm trying to help you.

Let me – .

– You're an impressionable young man. I could say anything
and you'd believe me.

Why do you believe me?

You want to believe so badly.

You do not yet know what it is. Do you?

Remember: this is true.

We're mostly on your side.

... We mostly want to help you.

... We want to help you *see*.

... Because we need you.

Without you we are nobody.

Here he comes.

He's coming down the stairs, from the attic again.

Is he sick?

Are you?

Are you going to do something now?

You could kill him.

He's coming down the stairs, from the attic again …

He's going to kill all of you.

Is he?

All of you. You deserve it.

I am he, and I'm not.

I've got a knife, I don't, I'm going to stab you in your beds. I'm going to do it. It will be a shame. Thank God! I've got a knife. I'm on the stairs.

You here?

Are you ready?

What are you doing?

I'm going to kill you if you don't kill me first.

I'm in the hallway now.

How are you going to stop me?

I'm right outside your door.

Are you there?

Are you listening to me still?

What are you going to do?

THE WINDOW

BROTHER

It's funny when I think about it. I had twenty minutes tops. I started
in the basement. My father had a work bench down there and my
first thought was: razor blades, right? Everybody thinks razor blades
first. Why? There was a girl in middle school who'd tried it once, and
for weeks afterward she had to wear these wrist cuffs made of gauze.
We called her Spidey, which was not the kindest thing considering her
father was a Vietnam vet who'd named her after his favorite drink.
Brandy. But:

My father kept an X-Acto knife on a corkboard, and I took it
down and unscrewed that tiny bolt that keeps the blade in place. You
know. And I pushed the blade up out of the handle and, you see, the
thing is: it was rusted. It was dull – he never used it. My father didn't
like to cut things, if he could help it. But he liked to be prepared to
cut. And I thought, This would be worse than a prison fight. I mean,
a crudely sharpened spoon would be less painful. And then I started
thinking about my highly problematic relationship to blood, and how
the last time I had my blood taken at the doctor's office (I thought I
had mono) I passed out and dreamed I was riding on a roller-coaster
with my twin brother beside me, screaming, the two of us, screaming,
and looking at each other, screaming, except I don't have a twin
brother. I've got a normal brother. He's younger than me and I don't
like him much.

I've always thought I might have had one – a twin. Because
maybe – I read this somewhere – maybe I had a twin like, you know,
in the womb? with me? my mother's womb? but he died off and I was
born alone. I'd absorbed him. Which would explain a lot. Namely my
suspicion that I've always been just about half-dead. There's a flicker
of something in my head, maybe, but the rest of me is like just meat.
You know. And I should mention I was seventeen. It was winter, there

was snow on the ground from the week before. And I thought about all that blood – there would be so much blood if I slit my wrists or my jugular or what have you, all over the floor – can you imagine cutting into your flesh like meat with a dull rusted blade? – if you could even use the word "cutting" it would really be more like gouging or goring or digging a trench in your flesh. There had to be a better option, right?

So I slid the razor back in the handle, re-screwed the little bolt and hung the X-Acto up on the corkboard again. You know.

And I looked for what else I had: paint thinner, Drano, wasp poison, which for some reason made me laugh. I could make a kind of toxic cocktail, cut it with milk – that wouldn't be too bad. But if there's one thing I hate more than blood it's vomit. And any of these chemicals, in any combination – let's be frank – you'd pass out and puke blood before it killed you. Or you'd pass out and they'd have your stomach pumped which is worse than vomiting. Or so I hear. – Or you get brain damaged. This friend of my friend's sister got brain damaged from trying to get high off a bottle of chloroform, when she passed out, and the whole thing spilled out on the rug around where her face was lying, and when she woke up she was stupid. Just like that. Couldn't talk anymore, she was mute. I didn't mean stupid before I meant dumb.

I thought about leaving a note but I didn't know what to say. Talk about pressure! Because I had no idea what my true motives were. Isn't that incredible? It's embarrassing now, pretentious even – I mean, I didn't know a single person who'd died at this point in my life. Not one single person. My parents, grandparents, teachers – all the old people I knew were still alive. And what did I have to complain about anyway? I didn't do drugs. Didn't have many friends, true, I don't know why. Didn't have sex. My father was a dick, my mother couldn't cook, I had to do my own laundry from the day I was ten – it was awful, really awful! I'd lost the junior class presidency that fall in a bloodless coup, which I'll admit came as quite a blow to me. I'd been class president for two years, so you could say I was almost popular in my own desperate way, but I didn't really enjoy the job, and it showed, and this Japanese kid named Bryan-with-a-Y ran on a ticket of exclusion and ousted me. His posters were in Japanese. Not that I'm bitter.

And since the election I'd been depressed …

I'm telling you – it's hilarious!

I went up to the kitchen and I put my head in the oven, just like Emily Dickinson. Or whoever. You know. I knelt on the floor and – not many people know how hard it is to fit a whole head inside an oven. I'm not tall, in fact my stature is what some people consider short. And in order to get my head in the oven I had to sort of lay myself flat on top of the oven door with my ass stuck out in the air and that door digging into my hipbone. My head was resting on that greasy oven rack – it smelled like chicken fat – and I tell you this so you can feel you're there. I want you to *feel* like you're here. *With* me. Like you *are* me. I want you to understand – because maybe by following me, step by step, you'll finally begin to figure it out.

I reached up above and behind my head and flicked the dial blind from zero to as far as it would go, and whoof the oven's up and I'm blown back and out and I hit my head on the way – I can't help it, I'm sorry, it's instinct! … My face was hot … but not even singed.

Not even singed!

I hadn't even considered that: instinct. What a novel idea. I mean it's not like I was a fragile old man. I have a body. Most people don't consider – they don't think about this, they think life is fragile, and it is, it is, but when you're young and healthy it's like your body is some incredibly vicious robust animal with a mind of its own, all its own, or no mind, just the animal, and you've got to fight the animal with your mind, with that little portion of mind that's left over after you take away the so-called reptile brain, the hypo-something-or-other, you know, the top of the spine that makes one breathe and one's heart beat fast or slow but beat no matter what all the time, not to mention all the darker, silent portions of the mind that have remained a mystery to modern science … You've got to be smarter than all that.

I could blow out the pilot light on the stove top, take deep breaths …

I could light my clothes on fire … This was a sort of protest, after all.

I picked up the toaster and hit my head gently with it, as a joke to myself. You know.

And I wished for a moment that I was an even smaller person, maybe the size of a canned ham, and I could just fit all of me inside the microwave and turn it on high, rotating – I would bubble. Maybe explode. The idea of exploding appealed to me very much …

My father kept a gun in a strongbox in his closet. I knew the combination because once he'd shown me the gun when he thought maybe I might turn out gay. It was a .22 rifle – he'd bought it for a hunting trip before I was born. He didn't like people to know he had it, he hardly ever used it. He cleaned it once in a while, alone in the bedroom on the bed with the door closed. You could tell by the way the house smelled after.

I unzipped the leather gun case. The gun was really surprisingly light. Like a shovel without a face. I went into the bathroom – my parents' bathroom, I don't why, it's sick – and put the toilet seat down, and I sat. I turned the gun around and pressed the barrel into the middle of my forehead. I reached for the trigger but the barrel kept sliding off, I was sweating so much. I would've put it in my mouth but I remembered what my dad once said about Hemingway. I took my shoes and my socks off, re-placed the barrel. I reached out with my toe, straining …

Click.

No bullets. I'd forgotten to load the fucking thing.

At this point you'd be forgiven for thinking I didn't really want to die.

I went back to the strongbox: no bullets in the strongbox. – What kind of father keeps a gun without bullets in the strongbox!

I put my shoes on and ran out to the garage for some rope. You know. Nice thick ship-rigging type rope that had been used maybe once by a neighbor to cut down this really large, really dead tree that hung out over our backyard, and the rope now hung coiled and sleeping on a corkboard, of course. – But just then my mother's station wagon came barreling down the street – damn it, why was there never enough time! – but I was back inside before she'd pulled in. Up the stairs to my room in the attic – there was a sturdy light fixture there.

I could hear their voices in the house below, my mother and my brother. She was confiding in him. I didn't really have anything against my kid brother except that my mother loved him more. No one likes to admit that but why not? Parents are people and people have affections, and my brother was universally adored. He was relatively good-looking, funny, athletic, tall. He was twelve. And my mother was always telling him things she really had no business telling, things about my father, a miscarriage, how depressed she felt as a housewife. You could bet money right now she was talking about me, about the report card she'd gotten in the mail today which wasn't exactly stellar – but who cared? I'd already made up my mind and it felt good. – What's wrong with your brother? she was probably asking him as I tied the rope from the garage into a noose and it smelled like pine – except I didn't know how to tie a noose – I mean, who does? unless you've got cause to hang something, unless you're a hangman, unless you're like this hopelessly fucked-up kid who tortures animals and I wasn't one of them. So I just kind of looped the rope around my neck once and tied a double knot, then lassoed the rest up over the sturdy light fixture, climbed up on my bed with my shoes on, and I prayed:

Please God let this work.

Then stepped off the bed, and – fell straight down.

Like something out of a movie. Like God was actively working against me here.

The rope had held tight and the light had crashed down on my head which had brained me but nothing too substantial. My mother below called up my name and my brother was sent up to look – I could tell by the way he bounded up the stairs, two at a stride. I pulled the rope up off my head – the skin was raw and scraped round the neck – .

What was I doing this for? Did I think I wouldn't die? That I'd die without dying? That there'd be a place I'd go after from where I could watch and explain things and say, See, this was your fault, or this part was your fault and this part was my fault, or even This is nobody's fault but entirely my own. It was like I was trapped in a room, a very dark room. And it was my room. I had gone into this room of my own accord. If I was trapped – and I was trapped – then it was my fault. Or it was nobody's fault. And as much as I wanted out I couldn't. I couldn't find the way out. Until I saw the window. I'm speaking metaphorically now. But it was like I was trapped in a pitch-black room and then sunlight outside lights up a window I didn't know was there.

And that's when I see it, as if for the first time.

Why hadn't I noticed it before?

Three stories down – that's enough, isn't it?

I open the window and I push up the storm screen. Cold air like water. My brother's voice from the bottom of the attic stairs, Mom wants to see you. I lift my leg up and through – I'm straddling the windowsill now – and my brother calls my name again as he climbs the stairs slowly.

I bring my other leg up, and through, and now I'm legs in cold, head inside, like a Ferris wheel. It's night now. Between my feet below the snow reflecting street- and moonlight. The neighbor's lights are on in every room and a shadow walks through a door frame. I duck my head outside. The moon sways and the trees bob, and it's all really so beautiful I can barely describe … I grip the sill for balance.

What are you doing? asks my brother. He's in the room behind me.

Get out, fag.

What are you doing in the window?

You know. You know what I'm doing.

I turn my head to look at him. And it's like I'm already dead. I'm looking back at him, who's alive. Or I'm looking at my own reflection, a younger, better vision of myself, happier, but almost my twin. – What's he thinking? What's he thinking right now about me? What is he going to think, years from now? Will he ever forgive me? And if he doesn't, will he ever just let it go?

Come back in, he says, I won't tell. He holds out his hand to me.

THEOTOKIA
(Hymn to the Mother of God)

1. Holy Anger

SON

A candle lay, a candle lay de lo.
A candle lay de lo, de loo.

And soon you'll know
what no man ever knows.

I am the holy anger
of the Son.

Disguised to mend God's broken mind.

My name
is Sacanala Vinda.

Sacanala Vinda!

Our name is something
we can't tell you,

something you can't know

yet.

2. There Is a Cave

YETI MOTHER

There is a cave

in the snowy heights

of the Himalayas.

Di lo la lo lo. Di lo la lo. Di lo la lo lo la di la loo. Ko lo ko ta.

I wait for you

in this dark warm cave

in the heights –

Ka re voo. Ka re ka re voo.

– in the heights

of the snowy Himalayas.

Ka va ka ne ko na.

I wait for you here.

Ka yee ka va tei vas sho ka. Ka yee ka va tei vas sho ka kas.

With my comfort,

with my love

I will guide you home.

3. How Could He Say This To Me?

MOTHER

Why
is he so angry at me?

He did everything I told him to.

Praying, all the time praying.

A good boy! A quiet boy! Nothing's wrong!

I would come into his room
at night
and pray over his sleeping body.

I was trying
to enshroud a child
in love.

When he came home
from the war
he held a photograph of a girl
I'd never met.

Then one day
when I was at church
he packed his suitcase and left,

and when he came home

he was no son of mine.

On Good Friday

when I was at church again

he broke the necks of the white doves on the roof.

He broke my statues of the saints.

He smashed all of my statues
and threw my crucifixes
in the trash.

And he said,

There will be no gods before me.

And he said,

I am the only begotten son of God,
and my name is
Jesus Christ.

How could he say this

to me?

4. To Me …

SON

to me to me to me

do this do this to me

to me to me to me

to to me

to me

to to tomorrow

to me to me tomorrow

tomb tomb ton ah ton ah

ton ga ton ga ton ga

don ga don ga don ga

don ga don ga don ga dong dong

dung

dung

dung

5. Dung!

YETI MOTHER

Dung! Dung! Dung!

Dung has self-contained energy!

Dung aids plants to grow!

Dung has a healthy smell that swells the air – *ah!*

where would the farmers be
without it?

The commode says,

Deposit in me.

And the Chinese man says, Honor mine today, indirect food
for tomorrow, most honored guest,

Dung!

Plowing-seeding-dunging-reaping –

Dung! Dung! Dung!

6. Song of the Yeti Mother

YETI MOTHER

Have you never heard the story
about the people who have yet to
be discovered?

Lu di a lu po!

Whose bodies are much stronger
than a human person's
body?

Vo ne har ko no mei, ko no hu!

Who are above the ape?

Who are the missing link?

Kio bo he, ko lo he lu he!

Who live
in the snowy

Himalayas?

Kio kio lu!

Who can lift a living yak
high above her head
and toss it like a sack of dung?

Who does all these things and more?

Vin du sa ka la!

I am your true mother,
Sakanala Vinda!

You cannot run
from me.

I va ka re, I va ka ra lu!

I have been waiting
here for you
in this dark warm cave
in the snowy heights of
the Himalayas.

Where blinding snow white skin and hair have not been stained
by sin,

only by the blood of the rodent rat
of sin!

Who love to eat
the raw red meat
of this rat of sin?

Who love to eat
the raw red meat

and shoot and stomp and squeeze and grip and bite
the living head of this rodent rat
of sin?

Come life,
Yeti life,
come life eternal.

Shake, shake out of me
all that is carnal.

Run life,
Yeti life,
run life eternal.

Stamp, stomp out of you
all that is carnal.

Run life,
Yeti life,
run life eternal.

Stamp, stomp out of you
all that is carnal.

All that is carnal.

All that is carnal.

7. That Sane Men Never Know

SON

So now you know

we are God's only children

and from Her holy anger
we must hide.

There is no cave ...

A candle lay,
A candle in your palm.
A candle lay,
A candle in your brain.

So many blessings
yet to come
that sane men never see.

There is no cave ...
There are no Himalayas ...

It is gone.

But where
am I

now?

I grope in the dark
and the people step on me.

I think, I hope.

But outside

who will I be

now?

THREE PANDEMIC VOICES

Unknown Caller

DAUGHTER: I've been told you're dying and I cannot
    see you. I didn't think I would want to
    say goodbye. I've told myself for decades
    that I wouldn't, when the time came, reach out
    in any way. Why, after escaping
    would I come crawling back to you simply
    because your time's up? When I was fighting
    for my life, five years ago now, touch wood,
    I didn't hear from you. Not a phone call
    or a letter, email, text. And I know
    you knew. So why tonight am I tempted
    to call you? I guess there's always the hope
    of a juicy deathbed confession. Like:
    Your father wasn't really your father.
    As I've long suspected. Or fantasized.
    Or you were abused as a girl – something
    to explain how you were. Or another
    kind of confession: an apology
    for not loving me. But they're telling me
    you're well past the point of being able
    to speak. Maybe you will have to listen
    to me, then. Finally. You're my captive
    audience. If I choose to send this. Well,

to begin with I would like you to know:
I don't hate you. I never hated you
anyway before, except in response
to feeling hated by you. For reasons
I've spent my life trying to decipher.
I did love you. I once loved you fiercely
as children do. They have to. But with time
and distance, and therapists – I forgot
about you. More or less. But this morning
when my phone said Unknown Caller, I knew
it was you. Or a nurse calling for you.
I was shocked you were still alive! Because
over the years you'd become like this ghost
in my imagination. Remaining
the age you were the last time I saw you
or younger, about the age I am now.
And it's true I've caught myself daydreaming
from time to time, about getting in touch
again, calling you and you would answer
and we'd catch up, and you would be so proud
of me. That I've fought so hard for my life
  – this moment, now, but also what I've made
with my talent. Not that you ever cared
for truth, or beauty. But you would have to
respect my life: my semi-famous wife.
My books and prizes. All the many miles
I've traveled, the faces I've met, when you
never had any friends and barely left

the house. I've even imagined ringing
your doorbell and surprising you, shocking
you with the laughter of the granddaughter
you'll never know now. This is her picture
but I won't show it to you. Is that cruel?
I feel I should protect her. She's sleeping,
you're far away. And as it ever was,
I'm imagining. I'm imagining
standing beside my daughter in front of
the house where I don't live, where you don't live
anymore, either. We're waving to you
from the street. You're at your window, solemn
and silent. My daughter asks, Who is that?
and I have to answer honestly that
I don't know. But I forgive her. Goodnight,
Mom. I hope it's not too hard.

After Krapp

SELF: Happy birthday. "The awful occasion,"   *(Eats a banana.)*

as Beckett would've said. Well he did say

those words. In *Krapp's Last Tape*, a solo show

we've always wanted to perform. "Spooool"

– you see? But probably this is the closest

we'll get to that role now. The theatre's dead

for real this time. Like *Waiting for Godot*

but longer. Endless. Or haven't you heard?

Of course you haven't, you're safely ensconced

in the past. Whereas I have been reading

our old journals, from that wanderjahr when

we went backpacking and acting around

Ireland for a year, digging up our roots

or some bullshit like that. I can't recall

why I went, why I'm reading now – escape,

I suppose, both times. And I am hoping

to be able to watch this video

many years from now, so he can judge me

like I'm judging you: you are a stranger

to me now, a stranger with hair. So hard

on yourself! And others. Aspirations

and resolutions. Ah well. To "succeed,"

you keep writing. Artistically or what,

I can't tell. You find yourself disgusting

physically. Poor kid. As you keep track of

every single pence: a biro, some stamps,

an early dinner of vegetable broth
and baked potato. Diligently sick
with dread. This is where the drinking begins,
understandably. What would I tell you
if I could? Enjoy yourself. There's so much
you don't see coming. You can't. Like cancer
for one – one of several calamities
we've so far survived. Though again your hair
has not. – God, I loved that hair! And that girl
you were writing letters to in Vermont
with the anthracite eyes and wheat-gold hair
– well, you married her. You have a daughter
you love shamelessly. Not to spoil the plot
for you. So why am I reading your words
past midnight? What am I hoping to learn
from myself? – Here, let me read this to you
as you. An entry from our birthday now
a thousand years ago.   *(Dons a wig.)*

YOUNGER: My watch has stopped
so I don't know the time. Ah well. Today
I turned twenty-three. Theoretically
I'll read this "years from now," etcetera,
when I'm old, successful, fat and happy
and I'll laugh at myself. Stupid bastard.
But the real reason I'm writing this down
is to have somebody to talk to while
I'm waiting in the Christian Brothers School
for rehearsal to begin. Nobody

else is here. Not the cast. I hear children
down the hallway in the gymnasium
practicing karate. This theater smells
of coffee, and moss. There's a stone statue
of the Virgin Mother in the corner,
eyeballing me. A prayer on the wall
is speaking to my predicament: "God,
we ask you to comfort the destitute
in their many guises: the sick, the old,
the lonely." This is a memorable night
though I can't say why. The rain, the howling
kids down the hallway. And somehow I sense
I'll never leave this room, the theatre, and
this loneliness I've struggled to evade
is in reality my – what? My what?
It doesn't matter. Suddenly I see
I've been holding onto the past, Father
and his rages, Mother's bruises, fearful
of losing. But losing what? I believe
that any loss will better me, whether
that is true or not. It's time I wrap up.
I hear the other actors arriving,
I have this feeling of great beginnings,
I must tell myself, and I must listen:
You'll be all right. Give it time. Then more time.
You are just beginning to discover
your true voice.

Night Walk

MAN: Just close your eyes and listen. Leave the phone
on the pillow and try to fall asleep
if you're able. I know it's not easy
having me gone, so far away from you,
but I'll be home soon, I promise. I'm sick
but I'm all right, I feel all right, but you
and others like you, and old people too
 – this is a sickness that would be too hard
on your body. So we're being careful,
your mother and I. And in a few weeks
I'll be home. Shall we imagine the night
or early evening when you'll be walking
outside with your mother, when everything
has gone back to normal – when you notice
a star. But blinking, like my eyes, blink-blink,
so you know it's an airplane, and it's me
inside. And that's why you're awake, because
you're waiting up for me. I like the night,
you say. Why? Because people are outside
talking and going places. Your mom says,
Do you know those ladies? One of them said,
Hello darling. They must be some neighbors
we've never met before. Does that big boy
know you? His bike has a light he's proud of.
A full moon's rising. A baby's crying
because she's tired. Are you tired? Do you see

another airplane is landing? By now
I'll be in a taxi and I'll be home
before you know it. You hear the sparrows
singing in the palm trees. Girls are going
to a party. They're wearing hula hoops.
Can you believe how dark it's got? It's fine,
you'll sleep late in the morning, Mom tells you.
Oh look – her phone dings – Daddy's texting that
he's at our door but he's locked out because
he forgot his key. Silly, silly man!
He's walking this way now, he'll meet us here
on the corner. What are you going to do
when you see him? You say: I'll run to him
and he'll pick me up and kiss me. Then what
will you say after he's done kissing? Hi,
giraffe. And what else? I got new cat shoes.
And what else? I went on a night walk! – Look,
here I come walking down the street to you,
my darling. Run to me. Oh, how I've missed
holding you.

AFTERWORD

These monologues span half my life, and the entirety of my
professional life; the earliest piece was written, I believe, in 1997; the
most recent only a few months ago. They are orphans and outcasts,
for the most part, as poetic monologue-plays of variable lengths have
never been a valuable commodity in the American theatre. But they
took the form they wanted. Some have been produced a few times
here and there; at least two have never been performed nor shared
publicly until now.

Speaking of histories: *The Angel in the Trees* premiered with
The Play Company at Manhattan Ensemble Theatre in New York
City, directed by Mark Armstrong with Jessica Dickey as Madeline.
It was previously published in the *St. Petersburg Review* (issue 8 1/2)
and in the anthology *Our Haunted World* (Whitlock Publishing, 2013).
Boxing the Compass premiered at Brown University in Providence,
Rhode Island, directed by the playwright with Iris Bahr as Constance,
Max Finneran as Peter, Lucas Fleischer as Morgan, and Miriam
Silverman as Maeve. *Am Lit, or Hibernophilia* was commissioned by
Keen Company and first presented at the José Quintero Theatre in
New York City, directed by Andrew Dickey with Daniel Gerroll as
Joe; the play subsequently premiered at Ensemble Studio Theatre's
Marathon of One-Act Plays in New York City, directed by Kevin
Confoy with Tom Bloom as Joe. *The Window* was commissioned by
and performed at Primary Stages in New York City in an evening of
short pieces entitled *Moments of Bliss*, directed by Tyler Marchant with
James Urbaniak as Brother. *Theotokia (Hymn to the Mother of God)*, the
libretto for composer Jonathan Berger's opera, was first performed at
the Spoleto Festival USA by Dawn Upshaw, directed by Berger, and
is inspired in part by *The Three Christs of Ypsilanti* by Milton Rokeach.
The opera premiered as the first act of *Visitations: Theotokia & The War
Reporter* at Stanford Live (Stanford University, CA, in a Beth Morrison

Projects and Stanford Live co-production) and at the Prototype Festival (in a co-presentation with Roulette) in Brooklyn, New York, directed by Rinde Eckert and performed by Melissa Hughes, New York Polyphony, and the St. Lawrence String Quartet. *Visitations: Theotokia & The War Reporter* was commissioned by the National Endowment for the Arts and The Andrew W. Mellon Foundation. *Unknown Caller* and *After Krapp* were commissioned by the *24 Hour Plays: Viral Monologues*, and premiered online as performed by Jessica St. Clair and Evan Handler respectively.

I wish to express my heartfelt thanks to the artists listed above, and to the countless other individuals involved in these productions; to George Spender and Salamander Street for giving these pages a book as a home; to my agent Beth Blickers, a steadfast and nurturing presence for me these twenty-plus years; to the Tennessee Williams Residency at the University of the South (Sewanee), where several of these monologues were written; to the Thomas J. Watson Foundation for a year's worth of independent study in Ireland when I was young and painfully impressionable; and most emphatically my everlasting thanks is due to my wife, Jessica St. Clair, who continues to inspire my admiration and my love.

D O'B

Los Angeles

October 2020

First published in 2020 by Salamander Street Ltd.
(info@salamanderstreet.com)

ISBN: 9781913630560

Cover image: Bill Jackson Photography (www.billjackson.photography)

Printed and bound in Great Britain

10 9 8 7 6 5 4 3 2 1